TEMPEST

a
screenplay

TEMPEST

a
screenplay

by

PAUL MAZURSKY
&
LEON CAPETANOS

PERFORMING ARTS JOURNAL PUBLICATIONS
NEW YORK CITY

LIBRARY OF CONGRESS CATALOGING IN PUBLICATION DATA
Tempest: A Screenplay
Library of Congress Catalog Card No.: 82-81975
ISBN: 0-933826-40-0 (cloth)
ISBN: 0-933826-41-9 (paper)

Design: Gautam Dasgupta

Printed in the United States of America

Publication of this book has been made possible in part by grants received from the National Endowment for the Arts, Washington, D.C., a federal agency, and the New York State Council on the Arts. Additional support from Columbia Pictures is gratefully acknowledged.

for Betsy, Meg, and Jill
Paul Mazursky

to Kathy
Leon Capetanos

<u>Preface</u>:

When the opportunity to publish the script of *Tempest* arose, the question was do we rewrite the descriptions and film terminology so that it is easier for the reader or do we leave the shooting script as it was originally written. The decision was to go with the shooting script. As you can see, it's not fancy. Indeed there are certain shorthands, brevities. But we felt that it would be more interesting for the rather sophisticated movie audience of today to read an actual shooting script rather than one specially written for publication.

Paul Mazursky
Leon Capetanos

FADE IN:

EXT. SEA—AERIAL VIEW—DESERTED ISLANDS—DAWN

(*First light . . . mist . . . slowly rising and revealing an island in the Mediterranean . . . a lovely silence is heard.*)

EXT. ISLAND

(*CAMERA sees details . . . orange trees . . . sleeping goats . . . a few old houses scraped bare by the elements. Simple. Beautiful. SOUND OF SNORING is heard.*)

EXT. STONE TOWER—MEDIUM SHOT OF PHILLIP DIMITRIOUS

(*Mid-to-late-forties . . . close-cropped, gray hair . . . a small gray dog (Nino) sleeps on his chest, his wet nose next to Phillip's nose. They are the Snorers. Phillip is sleeping on an old deck chair. An open book lies on the ground. A bucket of grapes stands next to the book. A black umbrella gives protection from the sun.*)

WIDE SHOT—COVE

(*We see that the tower is on one side of the wondrous white-pebbled cove. A hundred yards or so across the way, high on the other side of the cove, is an old stone cottage. Bright colored banners wave incongruously from the roof. A modern solar element is seen. A fine telescope is on the terrace of the triple leveled cottage. Newish ceramic bells wave in the breeze. A pet, white goat is tied to an olive tree in front of the cottage. A strange combination of the old and the new.*)

CLOSE-UP—PHILLIP

(*Twitching in his sleep. CAMERA MOVES RIGHT TO HIS EYES.*)

EXT. TOWER

(*As Phillip suddenly wakes from his dream. The gray dog yelps and leaps.*)

PHILLIP:
Son-of-a-bitch, what I wouldn't do for a different nightmare! . . . You had
the dream too, didn't you Dog? (*Calls to house across the cove.*) Aretha Honey
. . . Honey, this is important . . . Aretha . . .

INT. COTTAGE BEDROOM

(*Aretha, tanned, about thirty, wearing panties and a T-shirt, sleepily wakes up. We
HEAR Phillip shouting about his dream. Aretha wearily steps out onto the terrace.*)

EXT. TERRACE

(*As Aretha emerges, yawning. Her terrace is directly across from Phillip's tower. They
have to shout at each other to converse.*)

PHILLIP:
I had the dream again and the dog had it too.
ARETHA:
That's wonderful. Maybe it'll be on the six o'clock news, sweetheart. If only
we had the six o'clock news.
PHILLIP:
You look so good . . . How did you sleep?
ARETHA:
Are you kidding? Phil, separate bedrooms is one thing. But this is ridiculous.
PHILLIP: (*Starting down from his tower.*)
What's for breakfast?
ARETHA:
Coffee. Feta cheese. Bread. Feta cheese. And for a change of pace, a nice feta
cheese omelette.

(*By now, Aretha has strolled back into the cottage.*)

PHILLIP:
Come on, Nino. Let's take a piss.

INT. COTTAGE

(*Aretha smiles and starts to hum a modern tune. She goes down a stairway to the lower
level. The kitchen is old and beautiful. On the walls are garlic strands, drying cheeses, oc-*

topus skins, herbs, flowers.)

EXT. WHITE-PEBBLED BEACH

(*As Phillip, happy to be alive, strides across the beach, followed by Nino.*)

PHILLIP:
It's all here, Nino. Beauty, inspiration, magic and serenity.

STAIRS UP FROM COVE TO COTTAGE

(*As Phillip takes the steps two at a time.*)

PHILLIP:
Not to mention silence, amazement, intimacy and enchantment.

(*By now Phillip reaches the doorway of the cottage and is met by Aretha. He kisses her on the cheek.*)

PHILLIP:
Let's get cracking, kiddo. We've got a busy day. We have a lot of work to do on the theatre.

(*Aretha prevents Phillip from taking another step and rubs up against him.*)

ARETHA:
How about some work on my theatre?
PHILLIP:
Let's see how the day goes.
ARETHA:
I've forgotten what it's like to be sad after sex.

(*They go through the cottage and out onto the front terrace. There, under the shade of an olive tree, a table is set for breakfast. Dog barks happily at the pet goat. Phillip washes his face in a bowl of water. It's all very beautiful and rustic. Until we HEAR the SOUND OF PUNK MUSIC. It comes from a cassette carried by Miranda, who has just stepped out onto the terrace. She is fifteen, pretty, spunky, wears blue-jean cut-offs, zories, a halter and almost always carries her cassette player.*)

MIRANDA:
Morning, Dad . . . Morning, Aretha.
PHILLIP: (*Can't stand the music.*)
I had the dream again. Could you please lower that, honey? (*She lowers it.*) I

had the dream again.
MIRANDA: (*Munching a piece of bread.*)
I dreamt I was smoking a joint at a Go-Go's concert.
PHILLIP:
I want you to have a good breakfast. We have a lot of work to do today.
MIRANDA:
I'll meet you after my swim.

(*He goes to kiss her, but Miranda is already gone. Dog sprints after her. By now, Aretha is pouring coffee.*)

PHILLIP:
What's with her?
ARETHA:
It's called puberty.

(*Phillip bites into a piece of bread and thinks about what Aretha has just said. The goat baas. Phillip tosses the goat a piece of bread. Goat munches bread.*)

EXT. BEACH . . . CASETTE PLAYER ON ROCKS (SOUND: ROCK MUSIC)

(*Miranda, now naked, dives into the sea. She jumps up and down like a dolphin, her movements syncopated to the rhythm of the music.*)

ANGLE ON BUSH

(*Hold on bush for a moment. Then bush moves about five feet. It's magical. Then bush moves again. CAMERA MOVES TIGHT TO BUSH. We see enormous eyes, filled with desire. We HEAR grunts and sighs. This is Kalibanos.*)

KALIBANOS:
Ooooo . . . perfecto . . . some body . . . Double your pleasure . . . double your fun.

WATER—MIRANDA

(*As she comes to the water's edge, stretching for a moment to dry her hair in the sun.*)

BUSH

(*As it scurries closer to the water. You can feel the bush's passion by the pace it moves. It's clear now that Kalibanos has fashioned this portable bush to spy on Miranda.*)

ANGLE ON EYES

KALIBANOS:
Come on, baby. Let Kalibanos woo your poo.

ANGLE ON DOG

(*Sniffing at a wing-tipped cordovan shoe. CAMERA MOVES UP FROM shoe and we SEE all of Kalibanos. A Mediterranean-type. Thin, needs a shave. Wears an odd assortment of American-style clothes and some of his own things. Bermuda shorts, no socks, Hawaiian shirt, a wristwatch on both hands, a small visored hat that says "Guide" on the brim. The dog attacks him.*)

KALIBANOS: (*Jumping away from dog.*)
You dog . . . I kill you . . . I eat you.

ANGLE ON MIRANDA

(*Looks up and sees Kalibanos. She's angry.*)

MIRANDA:
Get him, Nino . . . I told you not to spy!

ANGLE ON KALIBANOS

(*A figure on the horizon chased by the tiny dog.*)

EXT. SLOPE NEAR FIELD—CLOSE ON KALIBANOS

(*Really afraid of the dog . . . running . . . right into Phillip. Kalibanos falls down. He is truly afraid of Phillip.*)

KALIBANOS:
Hey, Boss . . . Sorry. Scusa, scusa. Kalibanos kiss your feet.

(*He kisses Phillip's foot again and again.*)

PHILLIP:
Stop it!
KALIBANOS:
Kalibanos run because he saw scorpion. Hey, Boss, you need new shoes . . . I got a good deal on shoes, Boss. Italian loafers . . . smuggle . . . I sell you cheap.
PHILLIP:
Were you spying on Miranda?
KALIBANOS:
No. Not Kalibanos. He respect the Boss' daughter.

PHILLIP: (*He means this.*)
If you touch her, I'll kill you.

(*The men look at each other. Kalibanos drops his act for a split second.*)

KALIBANOS:
Later we go fishing. We catcha some eight legs, Boss.
PHILLIP:
And don't call me Boss.
KALIBANOS: (*Back to his act; voice drops an octave.*)
Sure thing Boss!

(*Kalibanos salutes and hurries away . . . Phillip picks up the dog.*)

EXT. FIELDS

(*Crimson flowers. Light just coloring the meadow. Phillip talks to dog as they stroll.*)

PHILLIP:
Isn't this place . . . so perfect? Man in his element. Harmony. Balance. You know what Lao Tse said, don't you? "Nature. It speaks true, why not man?"

(*Dog begins to yelp. He sees a white goat. Phillip puts down dog. Dog chases after goat.*)

(*NOTE: CAMERA MOVES CLOSER AND CLOSER TO Phillip. As it does so: SOUNDS of a city are heard. Horns, taxis . . . till we are CLOSE ON Phillip.*)

DISSOLVE TO:

EXT./INT. TAXI (NEW YORK CITY)—NIGHT

(*FIRST FLASHBACK. Phillip, wearing a tuxedo, in rear of cab. Miranda, fourteen, sits in the middle. On other side is Antonia, Phillip's wife, a lovely looking woman of about forty-two.*)

PHILLIP:
I hate New Year's Eve parties.
ANTONIA:
You say that every year and ten minutes after we get there you're the one who doesn't want to leave.
PHILLIP:
Those are parties with people we know.
ANTONIA:
Everyone living will be at this party.

PHILLIP:
Everyone dead will be at this party. It'll be noisy and pretentious and very, very nervous.
ANTONIA:
Phillip. We are noisy and pretentious and very, very nervous.
MIRANDA:
Will you two quit it, please?

(*Silence.*)

PHILLIP:
. . . We could have watched Guy Lombardo on television.
ANTONIA:
Guy Lombardo is dead.
PHILLIP: (*Surprised.*)
Really?

(*She nods.*)

PHILLIP:
That's sad.
MIRANDA:
Who was Guy Lombardo?

INT. NEW YORK TOWNHOUSE

(*Incredible mob. Disco, sexy, everyone in New York is there. Woody and Barishnikov are seen. Mailer is flirting with Bella Abzug. Kissinger is laughing at something Gore Vidal has just said. Phillip and Antonia are in the food line. Miranda is ogling the celebrities.*)

MIRANDA:
I just saw John Travolta
PHILLIP:
Who's that?
MIRANDA:
John Travolta!
PHILLIP:
Give him my best.
ANTONIA:
Here comes Alonzo.
PHILLIP:
A perfect way to end the year.
ANTONIA: (*For the first time really pissed.*)
Enough, Phillip.

(*Alonzo is sixty. Incredible energy. Citizen Kane and Dino, with Howard Hughes' hypochondria. With him is Gabrielle something, a totally gorgeous French starlet who is coming out of whatever she is wearing. Nearby are Harry and Sebastian who we'll later know as Alonzo's lawyer and doctor.*)

ALONZO:
Antonia. Phillip. Welcome to my home. (*Kisses them.*) Happy New Year, my friends.
GABRIELLE: (*French accent.*)
In seven minutes is Happy New Year.
ALONZO:
This is Gabrielle. We met an hour ago and we are already in love.
PHILLIP:
Gabrielle. Alonzo. This is my daughter, Miranda.
ALONZO:
Bellissima.

(*He reaches to kiss Miranda on the cheek, but she pulls away.*)

ANTONIA:
They don't like to be kissed at her age.
ALONZO:
I understand. I have only a son. But all he *wants* to do is kiss. Well, Phillip. You are happy?
PHILLIP:
I'm hoping next year will be more fun.
ALONZO: (*To Gabrielle.*)
Phillip is a moody man. But he is a genius, so all is forgiven.
PHILLIP:
I ain't no genius, boss.
ALONZO: (*To Gabrielle.*)
You know the Alonzo building?
GABRIELLE:
Of course.
ALONZO:
Phillip designed it.
GABRIELLE:
Oh . . . I love architects.

(*Suddenly Miranda screams.*)

MIRANDA:
There's Woody Allen!

PHILLIP:
Who is Woody Allen?
MIRANDA:
Dad!
ALONZO:
Come Gabrielle. We say bonjour a Woody. (*To Phillip.*) Don't forget. We fly
to Atlantic City on Thursday.

(*Alonzo and Gabrielle move off.*)

MIRANDA:
Can I go with you?
PHILLIP: (*Dreaming.*)
Where?
MIRANDA:
Atlantic City. I could catch the shows. The Split Enz are there.
PHILLIP:
I'm afraid to ask who the Split Enz are.

(*Suddenly the horns begin . . . "Happy New Year" is heard everywhere. The band
strikes up Auld Lang Syne . . . Everyone begins kissing everyone else. Antonia kisses
Phillip. From the balcony, Alonzo and two hostesses begin to toss white feathers down to
the party below.*)

ANTONIA:
Happy New Year, darling.
PHILLIP:
What??
ANTONIA:
Happy New Year!

(*Phillip sighs, smiles and turns to Antonia and kisses her. Phillip puts arm around
Miranda and smiles.*)

PHILLIP:
Happy New Year, kid.

(*CAMERA MOVES IN TIGHT ON Phillip. Anguish. White feathers float past his face.*)

CUT TO:

EXT. YACHT

(*THUNDER. Lightning in the sky. A yacht. Yacht pounded by gigantic waves. Huge storm. Miranda screaming. Her face is under water. She is drowning. Suddenly it is Antonia drowning.)*

INT. PHILLIP'S BEDROOM—NEW YORK APARTMENT—DAWN

(As he sits up, startled . . . awakes from the dream. Antonia, lying next to Phillip, wakes up too. She sees the look on his face.)

ANTONIA:
A nightmare?
PHILLIP:
Yeah . . . A wet dream, you might say. Lots of water . . . You were there, somewhere.
ANTONIA: *(Deadpan.)*
What was I wearing?

INT. PHILLIP'S APARTMENT—BATHROOM

(He goes into the bathroom.)

PHILLIP: *(Calls.)*
You were on a yacht. Then you were drowning.
ANTONIA: *(Calls.)*
Bring me a glass of water, please.

(Phillip looks into the mirror as he fills a glass of water. He stares at his own image. Squints. Sees a white hair on his chest. Plucks it out. He winces.)

BEDROOM

(Phillip hands the glass of water to Antonia. She drinks it.)

ANTONIA:
I had a long talk with a producer at the party.
PHILLIP:
Who?
ANTONIA:
You wouldn't know him. Terry Bloomfield . . . Oh yeah, you met him at the party with his wife, when we first went in. He asked me if I wanted to act again.
PHILLIP:
And?
ANTONIA:
I think I do. It's a comedy. Right here in the city . . . Why not?

PHILLIP:
That sounds good.
ANTONIA:
I'm picking up a script tomorrow.
PHILLIP:
Good . . .
ANTONIA:
Fidel Castro.
PHILLIP:
Good . . . What?
ANTONIA:
Have you heard one word I said?
PHILLIP:
Yeah. Fidel Castro wants you to do a play and you're picking up a script tomorrow.
ANTONIA:
You're full of shit, you know that?
PHILLIP:
I heard everything! Terry Bloomfield! The producer! It's a comedy.

(*He grabs her. They roll over. He pins her. He kisses her. She kisses him back. They hold each other.*)

ANTONIA:
This is a big thing for me. I'm nervous.
PHILLIP:
We're all nervous.
ANTONIA:
Aside from the fact that you're crazy, why are *you* nervous?
PHILLIP:
Because I am now a very old person.
ANTONIA: (*Suddenly.*)
And me?
PHILLIP:
You're very, very beautiful.
ANTONIA:
Thank you. You're pretty cute yourself, even for an old guy . . . I have to pee.

(*She gets up and goes to the bathroom.*)

QUICK CUT TO:

EXT. ATLANTIC CITY CONSTRUCTION SITE—DAY

(From high angle see bare beach, ocean, and the rusted framework of a construction site. Down below, amidst the abandoned cranes, and the giant derricks, we see Alonzo's Rolls Royce pulling in. From the POV of the moving car we drive under the beams and come to a stop. Mackenzie, a tall, ruddy man in his forties, walks to the Rolls. Alonzo, Phillip, and Harry Gondorf, Alonzo's attorney, get out of the limo. The chauffeur opens the door for Alonzo. Alonzo looks up at the site, livid with rage.)

MACKENZIE:
Morning, Mister Alonzo. Mister Gondorf. Hello, Phil.
PHILLIP: *(Likes Mackenzie, shakes hands.)*
Good to see you, Mackenzie. How's Jeanette? The kids?
ALONZO: *(Pacing under the beams.)*
Rust! Rust! The beams are rusty! *(To Mackenzie.)* What the hell is this? What are you people doing to me?
MACKENZIE: *(Calmly.)*
Sorry, Mister Alonzo. I didn't make the strike.
ALONZO:
I'm sick and tired of it! Between the taxes and the labor and the strikes it doesn't pay to own a casino. Will we make our schedule?
MACKENZIE:
We'll try, sir.
ALONZO: *(Flipping.)*
Try? Try is weak! I want to hear the croupiers by the New Year.
MACKENZIE:
Long as we don't get labor problems we've got a shot.
ALONZO: *(Looking up at the beams.)*
I want this to be the greatest casino ever built. Every floor named after a Roman emperor. Every suite named after a poet.
PHILLIP:
What? No Gods???

(Alonzo suddenly turns to Phillip. In a split second, he loses his rage and begins to smile.)

ALONZO: *(Crossing to Phillip.)*
Perfetto. Perfetto. We name the dining rooms after the Gods. You are a genius, Phillip.

(By now, Alonzo has his arm around Phillip and they stroll out from under the beams. Mackenzie and Harry follow.)

PHILLIP:
That's why you pay me the big bucks, boss.
ALONZO:
But you are becoming a bitter bastard. Peevish, childish, silly . . .

PHILLIP:
I agree.
ALONZO:
You are a typical American. You want to stay a boy. Impossible. Also, stupid.
Boys don't have half the fun we have . . . Boys are nervous. They don't know
who they are yet, they are mostly broke and they make love in the back of very
small sports cars. (*He sneezes.*) Son of a bitch! I'm catching a cold. (*Goes to
Mackenzie.*) Hey, Mackenzie, how are we going to heat this place?

(*As Alonzo and Mackenzie talk about the heating problems, Phillip moves away and stares
up at the girders. He sees a figure standing high up on one of the girders. It is himself.*)

GIRDER

(*Phillip falling down and down and down . . .*)

ANGLE ON PHILLIP

(*Watching himself fall in his daydream. He shudders. Phillip turns to the others.*)

PHILLIP:
I quit.

INT. LOBBY—ATLANTIC CITY HOTEL

(Alonzo, Phillip and Harry Gondorf, Alonzo's folksy, fiftyish attorney . . .
hurrying through the lobby. Lounge music . . . gamblers . . . the usual Atlantic City.)

ALONZO:
Tell him what I'll do to him, Harry, if he quits.
HARRY: (*Very affable.*)
Sue you. Make it impossible for you to work anywhere else. Probably send
some goons around to break your kneecaps. Live up to your contract, Phillip.
PHILLIP:
Screw my contract.
ALONZO:
Is a boy! (*Sneezes.*) Turn down the air-conditioning!
HARRY: (*To a Guard.*)
Turn it down.
GUARD: (*Almost salutes.*)
Yes sir.

INT. LOUNGE—ATLANTIC CITY HOTEL

(*They enter the lounge. A chubby, middle-aged comedian is doing his turn. His name is Arnie Trinc. We hear his jokes as the trio approaches.*)

PHILLIP:
Write it off as a mid-life crisis. I don't feel like building any more slums.
ALONZO:
It will be the most fantastic casino ever built and you know it, Phillip.
PHILLIP:
Do you want me to beg?
ALONZO:
A contract is a contract. Is a moral obligation. (*Sneezes.*) Turn down the air-conditioning!!!
TRINC:
Well, as I live and breathe, ladies and gentlemen, it's out founding godfather, Alberto Alonzo.

(*The band plays the theme from "The Godfather."*)

TRINC: (*Hums.*)
They're playing our song, Alonzo . . . Speaking of elephants, did you hear about the guy who crossed a hooker with an elephant? He's got a 2000-pound blond who puts out for peanuts.

(*No laughs from the 15-20 odd patrons. But Alonzo roars with laughter.*)

TRINC:
Did you hear about the Polish cruise? Eleven days and two nights. What about the guy who held up the Bank of Israel? He got away with $300,000 in pledges.

(*Alonzo can't stop laughing.*)

ALONZO: (*To Harry.*)
I don't know why, but he makes me laugh. Buy his contract.
HARRY:
For how long?
ALONZO:
For life. Laughter is never cheap.

(*They exit.*)

EXT./INT. LEAR JET—DAY

(*The bedroom in Alonzo's private jet. The usual fancy accessories, but there is a certain*

Mediterranean feeling in the decor. Dr. Sebastian, a red-haired man in his late forties, is taking Alonzo's blood pressure. Sebastian is homosexual and wears a toupee.)

ALONZO:
Well?
SEBASTIAN:
Pressure is a little high, but nothing dangerous. You may have the beginning of a slight cold. But, really, you're fine.
ALONZO:
I'm fine, eh? Then why do I feel so lousy.
SEBASTIAN:
Sixty hard years. I'm not a magician.
ALONZO:
If you were a good doctor you'd find something wrong.

(Sebastian exits the bedroom and joins the others. Phillip, Harry and Trinc are having a drink.)

HARRY:
Dr. Theo Sebastian, meet Arnie Trinc. He's our resident comedian.

(They shake hands.)

TRINC:
You make 'em cry. I make him laugh. Did you hear the one about the German couple . . .
SEBASTIAN:
Yes, I know that one, it's a particular favorite of mine . . . How are you, Phillip?
PHILLIP:
Drinking too much, smoking too much, and generally feeling tense.
SEBASTIAN:
Sounds just like me.
PHILLIP:
How long have you been working for Alonzo?
SEBASTIAN:
This is the end of my five-year contract.
PHILLIP:
Are you going to renew?
SEBASTIAN:
Well, my stethoscope says no, but my bank account says probably yes. I have expensive fantasies.
PHILLIP:
And you, Harry?

HARRY:
I'm on for life.
TRINC:
Same as me, Harry. You know the definition of Jewish foreplay? . . . Two hours of begging.

(*Alonzo emerges from his room. Gets a scotch from bartender. Phillip smiles, the others don't. He gets up to refill his drink.*)

TRINC:
I don't think this is my room . . . with my luck he'll ask me to chip in for gas.
ALONZO: (*Calls to Phillip.*)
Hey, genius, grab a seat.

(*Phillip sits next to Alonzo.*)

ALONZO:
So . . . you having trouble at home?
PHILLIP:
Why?
ALONZO:
When a man as smart as you is jumpy, it's usually got something to do with his bedroom.
PHILLIP:
My bedroom is fine.
ALONZO:
She getting the headaches?
PHILLIP: (*Laughs.*)
No. I'm getting the headaches.
ALONZO:
Maybe you need something very young. Not that your wife isn't a beautiful woman. She certainly is very beautiful. But let's face it, sometimes a man needs new flesh.
PHILLIP:
You have a wonderful way with language.
ALONZO:
Yes, I talk straight.
PHILLIP:
You do have the energy. How the hell do you do it?
ALONZO:
How do I do it? I know that every moment I have may be my last. So I'm in one big hurry.
PHILLIP:
Don't you ever get the urge to just relax? Hang out with your son?

ALONZO:
That's what Christmas is for.

(*Trinc walks over.*)

.

TRINC:
Did you hear about the Polish strip tease joint? . . . Put it on . . . put it on
. . .

(*Alonzo starts to laugh . . . then cough . . .*)

ALONZO: (*Coughing, laughing.*)
Crazy son-of-a-bitch makes me laugh . . . (*To Phillip.*) Remind me, I have to
talk to you about my mausoleum.

(*Harry and Sebastian help Alonzo off to his cabin. Phillip takes in the "mausoleum" bit
and finishes his drink.*)

EXT. ROOFTOP OF PHILLIP'S APARTMENT—DAWN

(*Phillip is looking through his telescope. [Same telescope as earlier seen on the island.] He
watches a man feeding his pigeons on the rooftop across the way. Miranda comes out, carrying the cat. Phillip turns away from the telescope.*)

PHILLIP:
Hi, sweetheart.
MIRANDA:
What are you looking at?
PHILLIP:
Pigeons. Did I wake you up?
MIRANDA:
No. I couldn't sleep. Maybe I should take some valium.
PHILLIP:
Hey . . . out of the question.
MIRANDA:
Why? You use it.
PHILLIP:
Because I said so—no. It's not good for you . . . How's school?
MIRANDA:
Exceptionally boring. Except for basketball.
PHILLIP:
I'll have to see you play.
MIRANDA:
There's a game Thursday. Against Taft. They're good. All black and seven

feet tall.
PHILLIP: (*Smiles.*)
Is that a bit of prejudice?
MIRANDA:
No. It's the truth. They're all black and seven feet tall.

(*They walk towards rooftop door. Phillip carries his telescope.*)

PHILLIP:
Are you having a good time, kid?
MIRANDA:
You're extremely philosophical for this early in the morning.

(*They go into the apartment, close rooftop door.*)

INT. KITCHEN

(*Antonia is making coffee. She sees Phillip and Miranda come down the stairway.*)

ANTONIA:
Anything wrong?
MIRANDA:
We couldn't sleep.
ANTONIA:
Oh . . . Want some breakfast?
MIRANDA:
I'm going back to sleep. If I'm not up by seven, would you wake me?
ANTONIA:
Please.
MIRANDA:
Please.

(*Miranda exits with an apple.*)

PHILLIP: (*In living room placing telescope down.*)
Oh . . . Goddamn . . .
ANTONIA:
Are you okay?
PHILLIP:
I want to quit. I want to get out. I've had enough.
ANTONIA:
What do you want to do instead?
PHILLIP:
I dunno . . . dream, wander.

ANTONIA:
Terrific. I want to work. You want to wander.
PHILLIP:
Bad timing, eh?
ANTONIA: (*Returning from refrigerator.*)
No, no . . . If you really want to quit, then you should quit.
PHILLIP:
Ah. But if I quit, then I won't have any more excuses, will I?
ANTONIA:
Phil? Are you not in love with me?
PHILLIP:
What the hell has love got to do with this?
ANTONIA:
I'm asking you if you care about me. Care about us. Not just you.
PHILLIP:
I don't need your guilt.
ANTONIA:
You haven't answered the question.
PHILLIP:
I care about you. I care about your work, I care about your happiness. I care.
But most of the time, I don't give a shit about anything.
ANTONIA:
Except yourself, you mean.
PHILLIP:
Yeah, that's right. You got it! (*He picks up a dish on the counter.*) I don't care
about these cheese things. They bore me. I don't care about this kitchen. I
hate these white walls. They're boring. (*He walks around the living room.*) I hate
this floor! I hate this vase. (*He lifts it and starts to smash it.*)
ANTONIA:
Go ahead. Break it. You don't like it, break it!
PHILLIP: (*Puts vase down.*)
I'm the king of high tech! (*Points at cat in chair.*) I hate this cat. I hate its
whiskers. I hate its fleas. And I hate you.

(*Phillip points at Antonia. He sees Miranda who has come back to witness the end of his
tirade. Phillip leaves.*)

PHILLIP: (*To Miranda.*)
Sorry. Sorry, kid.
MIRANDA: (*To Antonia.*)
What's the matter?

(*Antonia, in pain, shrugs and goes back into the kitchen.*)

INT. HOSPITAL EXAM ROOM

(*Phillip is on the treadmill, jogging . . . Tubes attached to his arms. Blood pressure sleeve on the other arm . . . Nurse, Doctor . . . Machinery . . . This is the thalium heart test. Looks scary. Nurse is calling out blood pressure figures . . . Phillip looks worried.*)

PHILLIP:
Is that good or bad?
DOCTOR:
Pretty good.
PHILLIP:
What do you mean, *pretty* good.
DOCTOR:
So far you've got a great heart, Mr. Dimitrious.
PHILLIP: (*Panting, smiles.*)
Call me Phil.
DOCTOR:
You let me know when you've had enough.
PHILLIP:
I could go for another hour.
DOCTOR: (*Smiles.*)
Yes, but we want you alive.

(*Phillip stops immediately.*)

PHILLIP:
Is something wrong?
DOCTOR:
Keep walking. Nothing's wrong.
PHILLIP: (*Smiles.*)
You don't have a cigarette, do you, Doc?
NURSE: (*Calls out.*)
One-ninety over one hundred.

(*They help Phillip down and take him into the X-ray room. They lie him down.*)

NURSE:
Doctor, there's an emergency phone call for Mr. Dimitrious.
DOCTOR: (*To the Nurse.*)
Put the call through . . .

(*The Nurse hands the phone to Phillip, who is now lying flat on his back.*)

PHILLIP:
Yes? . . . Hello, Harry. No, this is just a routine checkup . . . When did that

happen?

(*It's obviously bad news.*)

PHILLIP:
All right, I'll fly out tomorrow.

(*He hands the phone back to the Nurse.*)

NURSE:
You have bad news?
PHILLIP:
Yeah. A fellow named Mackenzie just died of a heart attack.

AERIAL VIEW OF ATLANTIC CITY—DAY

(*Seen from a helicopter . . . revealing Phillip and Harry sitting in the Alonzo company copter.*)

INT. HELICOPTER—HARRY AND PHILLIP

HARRY:
Mackenzie seemed like a good foreman . . . Did you know him well?
PHILLIP:
Not really. I liked him. A classy man. No bullshit. One of those guys who don't talk a lot who you can trust.
HARRY:
He'll be tough to replace, won't he?
PHILLIP:
You never stop working for Alonzo, do you?
HARRY:
That's not fair.
PHILLIP:
Do you?
HARRY:
No. I guess not.
PHILLIP:
What's he got on you?
HARRY:
Not a thing . . . Tell you something, Phil. The gangsters are everywhere. Business, sports, government. At least with Alonzo, it's out in the open.
PHILLIP:
. . . Maybe I'll go to an island and watch the sun come up.
HARRY:
The gangsters are on the islands, too, Phil.

(Phillip looks out the window. He sees the funeral procession on the road to the cemetery.)

INT. PHILLIP'S LIVING ROOM—NIGHT (RAIN)

(A party working nicely. Antonia and a half a dozen show-business friends. Murray is at the piano. Antonia and Miranda are finishing a song—"Ain't Misbehaving." Applause from the others, including Terry Bloomfield. It's all fun and warmth.)

ANTONIA:
Sounds like George Burns, just a bit?
PAUL:
You have a nice voice. She really has a nice voice.
CYNTHIA: *(An actress.)*
I hate the word nice.
PAUL:
. . . A sweet voice.
TERRY:
I hate the word "sweet."
MARK:
A tragic voice?
ANTONIA:
Yes, I'll buy that.

(They all laugh.)

CYNTHIA: *(To Terry.)*
All right Terry, tell us about the new play, or is that against the law?
TERRY:
No, it's a comedy . . . Paul knows—he's directing, let him tell you.
CYNTHIA:
Yeah, yeah???
PAUL: *(Joking.)*
It's rather like a cross between "Chorus Line" and "Macbeth."

(Laughter.)

MIRANDA: *(From kitchen.)*
We're studying "Macbeth" in school. Unbelievably boring.
MARK: *(To Terry.)*
So Terry, tell me, when are you going to do some Pinter or Pirandello? Something not so safe.
TERRY:
Safe? Safe? Listen, my friend, Terry Bloomfield has taken more chances with off-beat material than any producer on or off-Broadway. And I've lost more

money doing it than any producer on or off-Broadway.

BETSY: (*His wife.*)

You can say that again.

MIRANDA:

I saw something by Pinter on T.V. It was really boring.

MARK:

Pinter should not be seen on T.V.

MURRAY: (*Playing "As Time Goes By."*)

Is there any more pate?

ANTONIA:

Certainly. (*To Miranda.*) Mush, you should be in bed.

MIRANDA:

As soon as "Johnny Carson" is over.

(*Antonia serves the pate to Murray and starts singing the beginning of "As Time Goes By." The others join her. Phillip enters apartment . . . He sings a line and then trips, drunk.*)

PHILLIP:

Ah, a party. What are we celebrating?

ANTONIA:

Hello, Phil. You're home early.

PHILLIP:

It was a quickie funeral.

ANTONIA:

Are you drunk?

PHILLIP:

I'm working on it. Introduce me.

ANTONIA:

Oh yes. Murray, you know . . . And Cynthia doesn't need an introduction.

CYNTHIA:

Hello Phil . . .

ANTONIA:

Paul, Paul Fredericks . . .

PAUL:

Hi, I'm the director . . .

ANTONIA:

Mark, come here—I don't believe you know Phil. Mark is in the play . . .

PHILLIP: (*Shaking Mark's hand.*)

You can let go now . . .

ANTONIA:

And Betsy and Terry Bloomfield . . .

PHILLIP:

Aaah, hello . . . (*He kisses Betsy.*)

TERRY:
Hi, I'm Terry Bloomfield. We met New Year's Eve at Alonzo's . . .
PHILLIP:
Terry Bloomfield, you are the producer! Could I ask you . . . could, would you dance with me?
TERRY:
What?
PHILLIP:
Just say yes. Don't make it complicated.
TERRY:
Okay.
PHILLIP:
Would you sing? I can't dance without music.
BETSY:
Let's go home!

(*Phillip and an embarrassed Terry dance towards the kitchen. Phillip sees Miranda.*)

PHILLIP: (*Angry; to Miranda.*)
What the hell are you doing up?
CYNTHIA:
Why don't we call it a night . . .
TERRY: (*To Phillip.*)
Take it easy, take it easy.
PHILLIP:
What the hell is this kid doing up at one of these goddamned show business parties?

(*The others are clearly embarrassed and start to take their leave, heading for the front door.*)

TERRY: (*To Antonia.*)
You sure you'll be all right?
ANTONIA:
I'm sure. I'm sorry, I'll call you tomorrow Terry.
TERRY:
Wonderful party, Antonia. Thanks.
PAUL: (*To Phillip.*)
Goodnight, Phillip. I enjoyed your entrance, but the performance was a bit overplayed. (*To Antonia.*) Goodnight darling, ten o'clock tomorrow.
ANTONIA:
Goodnight, see you later guys.

(*They all exit. She closes the door, heads back into living room.*)

ANTONIA:
That was truly, uniquely disgusting.

INT. KITCHEN

PHILLIP:
I want the kid to go to . . .
MIRANDA:
I'm not the kid. Kids are goats.
PHILLIP:
Go to sleep.
MIRANDA:
I'm not tired.
PHILLIP:
She's got to go to bed!! Listen, I am the master of this house.
ANTONIA:
You're the one who should be in bed.

(*Lightning. Phillip and Antonia look up at the skylight. He smiles.*)

PHILLIP:
Tell it like it is, baby.

(*Immediately another flash of lightning as if in response to Phillip's statement. Phillip chuckles.*)

PHILLIP:
Yes, sir!
MIRANDA:
You're really rude.

(*Miranda shuts off T.V. and exits. Phillip walks into the living room, to the large windows, calls to the heavens. Thunder and lightning.*)

PHILLIP:
Once more, with feeling.

(*The entire living room is illuminated by a huge flash of lightning.*)

PHILLIP:
Show me the magic . . . show me the magic . . .

(*Frightened by his own power, he goes toward the bedroom.*)

INT. BEDROOM

(*Antonia puts on pajamas, crosses to bed.*)

PHILLIP:
Sorry.
ANTONIA:
So am I.

(*She sits on the bed and Phillip slides next to her, his head on her shoulder.*)

PHILLIP:
Problem is, I found a white hair. I plucked it out, but it grew right back.
ANTONIA:
Problem is, you need help.
PHILLIP:
Help.

(*He is asleep now, leaning on Antonia. Thunder, lightning . . . Antonia turns off the light.*)

CUT TO:

INT. GREEK COFFEE SHOP IN QUEENS (ASTORIA)—DAY

(*Phillip is having coffee with his father. The father is a spunky man of about seventy. Half a dozen Greek men are having coffee and chatting at other tables.*)

FATHER:
Your mother and I argued once a week. Just for pleasure. Small things. To buy a car or not? Why didn't I go to church more often? Too many backgammon games with the boys.

(*The cafe owner, a Greek man, comes over with the change for the bill.*)

FATHER:
Gus . . . Gus, come here. My boy had a fight with his wife.
OWNER:
Oh . . . did you hit her?
PHILLIP:
No.
OWNER:
Well, then it's not a fight.

(*He goes back to the counter.*)

ANGLE ON TABLE

FATHER:
You look like goat shit.
PHILLIP:
. . . Do you ever think of yourself as old?
FATHER:
It's relative. If I'm with Miranda, I feel I'm an old man, because she's just a little girl. If I'm with Nick Pappas, I feel like a spring chicken. Nick is pushing eighty.

(*They get up and exit cafe.*)

EXT. STREET—DAY

(*As they stroll, they talk. Lots of Greek shops . . .*)

PHILLIP:
And when you're with me?
FATHER:
I feel like father. Not old, not young. I say . . . well, here's my son Phillip. How is he doing? Is he making a living? Why doesn't he visit the old man more often? Things like that . . . Poppa stuff . . .
PHILLIP:
You're never confused?
FATHER:
I'm always confused. Always. I remember yesterday better than today. But that's life. Life is problems . . . life is joys . . . life is a joke . . . Hey, did you hear this one? What's Jewish foreplay?
PHILLIP:
Two hours of begging.
FATHER: (*Disappointed.*)
Aah . . . Nick Pappas told me that joke. I thought it was new . . . So you're in trouble, eh kid?
PHILLIP:
Yeah. The money and the power don't mean a thing.
FATHER:
And the family?
PHILLIP:
Antonia wants to work again. And Miranda watches us argue . . . It's great.

(*They continue walking, toward Off Track Betting parlor.*)

FATHER:
You got a girlfriend?
PHILLIP:
No.
FATHER:
She got a boyfriend?
PHILLIP:
No.
FATHER:
Well, wait . . . wait. Marriage is like baseball. It's a long season.
PHILLIP:
You're a funny man, Pop.
FATHER:
Yeah, I'm funny . . . Take a vacation. Go to Greece. Watch the grapes grow.
PHILLIP:
. . . Did you hear the one about the Polish strip tease joint?
FATHER:
Yeah . . . Put it on, put it on . . .
PHILLIP:
Who told you, Pappas?
FATHER:
No. Johnny Carson.

END FLASHBACK

CUT TO:

EXT. ISLAND—BACK IN THE CRIMSON FIELDS

(*Phillip smiles at the memory of his father's joke. He calls to Nino.*)

PHILLIP:
Come on Nino. Time to get to work.

(*Phillip and Nino walk down field.*)

EXT. THEATRE SITE

(*We see Phillip's amphitheatre—Kalibanos, Aretha and Miranda are busy building the theatre. Hillside location, trees . . . all in a beautiful valley near the sea. About ten rows of proposed seats are laid out in a semi-circle. Below, a circular area meant to be the stage. Kalibanos and a burro pull the pulley which delivers stones to Phillip who stands astride a platform. Aretha and Miranda are pounding rocks into place at the bottom of the hill. It is obvious that this is a daily ritual. It is very hot.*)

PHILLIP:
You're doing good work. Excellent work.

(*He walks across the "stage" to a ladder at the far end and climbs up, surveying the amphitheatre.*)

MIRANDA: (*To Aretha.*)
Did you ever dye your hair?
ARETHA:
Oh sure. I was a redhead once for three months. Why?
MIRANDA:
I was thinking of putting a pink and a green streak in my hair.
ARETHA:
I could do it . . . I used to work in a beauty parlor.
MIRANDA:
You did? What did you do?
ARETHA:
I was a manicurist. I've done everything . . . I taught school, ran a pottery co-op. This is my first job as a construction worker!
PHILLIP: (*From atop the ladder.*)
Yes . . . Acoustics perfect . . . (*Calls out.*) Feta . . .
MIRANDA: (*To Aretha.*)
. . . When did you have your first affair?
ARETHA: (*Carrying a large stone.*)
In high school. With the star of the basketball team. His name was Zucky Mazaris. He was about ten feet tall, very handsome. He taught me all about things like dribble and jump shot.
PHILLIP:
Bring more stones, Kalibanos.
MIRANDA:
I think I may die a virgin!

(*Aretha laughs. Kalibanos carries over an armful of rocks, drops them.*)

KALIBANOS:
Time for a fig break, eh, boss?
PHILLIP: (*Looks up at the sun.*)
Five more minutes.
KALIBANOS:
Maybe tourist boat come. Who's going to show the tourists the cave?
ARETHA:
Hey. When did we get to this island?
KALIBANOS: (*Counts in Greek.*)
Ena, Thia, Tria . . . I figure twelve full moons.

ARETHA:
A year, right?
KALIBANOS:
Yeah, one year.
ARETHA:
And how many tourists have there been?
KALIBANOS:
The fat English lady who look for the ruins and the Arab who look for oil.
MIRANDA:
What she's saying is it isn't likely there'll be any tourists today.
ARETHA:
Thank you.
KALIBANOS:
Okay, okay, okay . . .

(*He walks away and goes for his clarinet at the table, plays a shepherd's tune.*)

PHILLIP:
We're not tourists anymore.
ARETHA:
No, we're day laborers.
PHILLIP:
We're learning to live like humans.
MIRANDA:
Humans go to the movies. Humans buy clothes and go shopping. Humans get a piece of the action.
PHILLIP:
"Piece of the action"? Wher'd you get that talk?
MIRANDA:
I heard it on T.V. In the bad old days.
PHILLIP:
Well thank God . . . there's no such crap on this island!
ARETHA:
No . . . We've got sheep and goats . . .
MIRANDA:
Goats and pigs and . . .
ARETHA:
And rocks . . . we've got lots of rocks.
PHILLIP:
You can grab the next boat.
ARETHA:
What boat???
PHILLIP:
The boat—It's a row boat trip. Kalibanos, run her over.

(*Aretha throws down her gloves and hat in disgust.*)

ARETHA:
Okay . . . great . . . okay . . . that's fine.
PHILLIP:
All you have on your mind is sex.

(*As she marches past him, Phillip gives her a kick in the pants. She flails at him with both fists.*)

ARETHA:
Well, six months is a long time to do without.
PHILLIP:
I know. I know. But I now am consciously practicing celibacy.
ARETHA: (*Stunned, smiles.*)
. . . You are consciously practicing celibacy? You are looney tunes!

(*Kalibanos picks up the "Looney Tunes" phrase and starts making up a tune on the clarinet. Phillip and Aretha push each other around.*)

KALIBANOS: (*Sings.*)
Looney-tuney, tuney-tuney tuney . . .
Looney-tuney, tuney-tuney tuney . . .
Goats and sheep and octopipi . . .

(*Phillip now picks up the song and starts to dance. Kalibanos plays the clarinet in the same tune, then drops it, and joins in the dance, as do Miranda and Aretha. They form a line and dance around the stage of the amphitheatre. Finally they stop dancing and embrace.*)

PHILLIP:
Isn't this beautiful? Wasn't that a moment . . .
ARETHA:
It was a moment . . .
PHILLIP: (*Picks up Aretha.*)
Where else on this polluted globe would you experience something like that?

(*Phillip and Aretha disappear . . . Kalibanos looks at Miranda, who also turns to go.*)

MIRANDA:
That was pretty neat.
KALIBANOS:
Hey, psst, hey, kid . . . I got surprise.
MIRANDA: (*Suspicious.*)
No thanks.

KALIBANOS:
No, is good surprise, really. Is secret.
MIRANDA:
What's the secret?
KALIBANOS:
You promise not to tell boss?
MIRANDA:
I promise.
KALIBANOS:
I got T.V. in my cave.
MIRANDA:
What???
KALIBANOS:
Sony Trinitron. I trade four goats including my dear Alexander to Marco
from Sicily.
MIRANDA:
Show me!
KALIBANOS:
Yes . . . Go . . . Go.

(She leads the way up to his cave. Kalibanos watches her rear wiggle. He stares with awe.)

EXT. KALIBANOS CAVE—DAY

(As Kalibanos and Miranda climb up path, walk to cave entrance.)

INT. KALIBANOS CAVE—DAY

(Miranda and Kalibanos enter. Kalibanos' wardrobe (which was once Phillip's) hangs on pegs on the walls of cave. A twelve-inch portable Sony sits on a small table. Goats sleep on his bed.)

MIRANDA:
Does it work?
KALIBANOS:
Sure thing, pretty lady. Have a fig while I fix the aerial.

(Kalibanos hands Miranda some figs. He pushes up tin can attached to a stick.)

EXT. CAVE

(A modern T.V. aerial appears through the bushes on top of the cave.)

INT. CAVE

(Kalibanos runs to the set and clicks it on. Miranda is goggle-eyed. Flicks and noises from the set. Finally the sound clears up and a picture begins to form. Sound is the THEME SONG from "Gunsmoke." The picture is a dubbed Greek version of "Gunsmoke.")

KALIBANOS:
Good, eh?
MIRANDA:
Incredible.

(Kalibanos hurries to the wash basin in the other corner, smells shirt, then takes it off.)

KALIBANOS:
Ring around the collar . . .

(He splashes water all over himself, sprays his underarms and mouth with a breath spray.)

KALIBANOS:
Good to the last drop.

(He selects a robe, then changes his mind and puts on a jacket, saunters off. He returns to sit at Miranda's side, pretending to look at the T.V. show.)

KALIBANOS:
Some show, eh? Kalibanos not such a bad guy, eh? You like Kalibanos?
MIRANDA:
Have a fig.

(She tosses him a fig. He savors it.)

KALIBANOS:
. . . I would eat you like this fig.

(He sucks the fig and devours it. Miranda turns from the T.V.)

MIRANDA:
Can't you ever stop?

(Kalibanos looks hurt . . . almost a child.)

KALIBANOS:
You are sweet flower. I know you are only a kid. I am only kid, too.
MIRANDA:
First of all, you're not a kid. And second of all, I'm not a kid either.

KALIBANOS:
I want to touch . . . to kiss . . . to balanga you with my bonijoni . . .
MIRANDA:
You mean sex?
KALIBANOS:
I mean love . . . Agapi! . . . Hello.

(*He is suddenly the shy little boy on his first date. He takes her hand. Miranda feels strange . . . awkward . . . she lets him hold her hand.*)

KALIBANOS:
So soft . . . like bird feather . . .

(*He lifts her hand to his lips. She closes her eyes. He kisses her hand. Her eyes stay closed, almost in an invitation for him to go further. His other hand goes to her shoulder. She looks uncomfortable.*)

KALIBANOS:
Oh, my sweet . . . My sweet Goddess . . .

(*He kisses her on the neck. Her eyes open wide. She is shocked for a moment and then, as he tries to kiss her on the lips, she hits him smack on the nose. Kalibanos falls down.*)

MIRANDA:
You asked for it, pervert.

(*She runs out of the cave.*)

KALIBANOS: (*Tough again.*)
Beat it, kid!

(*She exits . . . he rubs his nose.*)

EXT. CAVE—DAY

(*Miranda runs out and down the hill.*)

EXT. PATH AND OLIVE GROVE—DAY

(*Miranda is upset. Something has touched her and it was more than Kalibanos' lips. She walks along the path.*)

MIRANDA:
I know I'm not a kid anymore. There's physical evidence to prove it . . . I still

feel like a kid though . . . Maybe I'm crazy like the rest of them. Maybe it runs in the family . . . I want to leave. I don't want to stay here anymore.

(*She stops to catch her breath. CAMERA MOVES INTO TIGHT CLOSE-UP as she speaks.*)

MIRANDA:
I want to go home. I want a Billy Joel album . . . tight pants . . . high heels . . . I want my cat . . . and a frozen daquiri.

(*CAMERA TIGHT ON MIRANDA.*)

SECOND FLASHBACK:

EXT. WEST SIDE HIGHWAY (NYC)—DAY

(*Miranda and Phillip are jogging.*)

PHILLIP:
. . . Frozen daquiris are too sweet and they make you dizzy.
MIRANDA:
It's the principle of the thing. I don't really want a frozen daquiri. I tasted one once and I almost barfed. But I'm not free to do what I want. Mom is . . . You are . . . I'm not.
PHILLIP:
We're not free. We're just older.
MIRANDA:
You can do what you want.
PHILLIP:
No, not really. I dream of things that I don't do.
MIRANDA:
Like what? Besides quitting your job.
PHILLIP:
My job is part of what I am. It's not that simple, dodo.
MIRANDA:
You think it's fun always asking for money?
PHILLIP:
Tough.
MIRANDA:
Kids have no economic base. We're practically hostages.

(*They've stopped jogging and are standing on the highway adjacent to the World Trade Center towers.*)

PHILLIP:
You watch too much television.

MIRANDA:
I do not—I read all the time. You always see me reading.

(Phillip suddenly stares. He sees something that shocks him. Miranda sees the expression on his face and turns to look at what he has seen.)

THEIR POV

(Antonia in a striking dress is escorted to a waiting limo by Alonzo. He laughs. She smiles. He kisses her hand as she gets into the limo.)

ANGLE ON MIRANDA AND PHILLIP

(Stunned . . . Miranda grows up at this moment. She turns and looks at Phillip.)

INT. LIVING ROOM—LATE DAY

(Antonia and Phillip are in the middle of an argument.)

ANTONIA:
I'm not in love with him.
PHILLIP:
He uses people like Kleenex, he blows his nose, then he throws it away . . .
ANTONIA:
Don't start . . . That'll be my problem from now on.
PHILLIP:
Hey kid, you want a divorce?
ANTONIA:
Yes, I do. I want my freedom.
PHILLIP:
You want your freedom? I'll throw you out the fucking window and you can fly straight down and take birdface with you . . .
ANTONIA:
Oh yeah, go ahead, do it, bigshot . . .

(Miranda has now come into the living room.)

MIRANDA:
If you're not in love with him, then how can you see him?
ANTONIA:
Were you listening to that?
MIRANDA:
Yeah.
PHILLIP:
She lives here. She might as well as hear everything.

ANTONIA:
Oh Mush . . . I didn't want you to get caught in the middle of all this.
MIRANDA:
Can't you go see a marriage counselor?
PHILLIP:
Yeah. Why don't we go see a shrink?
ANTONIA:
Don't show boat in front of our child . . . I don't want to live with your father anymore. And if he'd be honest, he'd tell you that he's not really interested in me.

(*Miranda goes to the couch.*)

MIRANDA:
But . . . He loves you.
ANTONIA:
Maybe. But he's not interested in me.
PHILLIP:
And Alonzo is?
ANTONIA:
I think so, yes.
MIRANDA:
I'm not going to live with you and that creep.

(*Antonia sits next to Miranda.*)

ANTONIA:
I'm not living with him. I'm just seeing him.
MIRANDA:
Are you sleeping with him?
ANTONIA:
Miranda, you can't ask me that kind of question.
PHILLIP:
That's a good question.
ANTONIA: (*To Phillip.*)
You shut up!
MIRANDA:
He's gotta be about a hundred years old.

(*Antonia puts her arms around Miranda. Miranda tries to break away, but Antonia holds her.*)

ANTONIA:
I love you, honey.

(*They are both crying now.*)

MIRANDA:
If you love me, then stay with Daddy!

(*Miranda jumps up and crosses to the window sill.*)

PHILLIP:
It's my fault, kid. Honest it is. The old man wants to wander.
MIRANDA:
You're not old.
PHILLIP:
Look, I'm wrong. Your mother's right. It's time to move on.
MIRANDA:
What about me?
PHILLIP:
You are loved.
MIRANDA:
Where are you going to go?
PHILLIP:
Greece, I guess.
MIRANDA:
Get back to your roots and that sort of thing?
PHILLIP: (*Smiles.*)
What a way to break a contract. Trade your wife for your job.
ANTONIA:
That's really low.
PHILLIP:
But it's true.
MIRANDA:
When are you going?
PHILLIP:
Now . . . tomorrow.
MIRANDA:
Me too.
PHILLIP:
I don't think . . .
ANTONIA:
No . . . you're not going. I don't want you to go.
MIRANDA:
I'm not going to live with you . . . (*To Phillip.*) It's summer vacation. Why can't you take me?
ANTONIA:
Take her Phillip. But just for the summer, okay?

PHILLIP: (*He nods.*)
Okay.
ANTONIA: (To Miranda.)
Just for vacation, okay?

(*The three of them sit in awkward silence.*)

CUT TO:

EXT. ISLAND—ANGLE ON PATH NEAR COVE—DAY

(*Miranda walking. Aretha is on the beach, pounding a rug on the rocks of the green water in the cove.*)

MIRANDA:
Hi.
ARETHA:
Hey Poptart, what'ya doing?
MIRANDA:
Kalibanos kissed me.
ARETHA:
What did you do?
MIRANDA:
I decked him . . . He's got a T.V. in his cave.
ARETHA:
He's got a T.V.? And he told you to come up and see the T.V.?

(*They are in the water now. They stomp around on the rug, and wash it in the old way.*)

MIRANDA:
We've got to convince Dad to go.
ARETHA:
It's not gonna be that easy sweetheart.
MIRANDA:
He's a little crazy, isn't he?
ARETHA:
Yeah . . . sometimes he is and sometimes he isn't. Mostly he is.
MIRANDA:
Then why do you stay?
ARETHA:
Folie a deux.
MIRANDA:
Explain.
ARETHA:
Okay . . . a French expression. One person is crazy, and he lives with a per-

son, the other person catches the nuttiness. Pretty soon, they're both nutty. That's "Folie a deux."
MIRANDA:
You mean love . . .
ARETHA: (*Affectionately pats Miranda on head.*)
Yeah . . .

(*CAMERA MOVES INTO A CLOSE-UP of Aretha; as she lifts the rug, it covers her face for a moment . . .*)

CUT TO:

FLASHBACK

EXT. HIGHWAY—ATHENS—DAY

(*Near the Harbor of Piraeus. Aretha wearing Khaki shorts, a T-shirt, and holding Nino (her dog) on a leash, waits for a bus. Phillip and Miranda are in the front seats of a jeep.*)

MIRANDA:
Look at that great dog.

(*Phillip pulls to a stop.*)

PHILLIP:
Miss . . .
ARETHA:
Yeah.
PHILLIP:
Where are you going?
ARETHA:
Athens . . . but if that's inconvenient, Brooklyn.
PHILLIP:
Come on, get in.

(*Aretha and Nino get in.*)

PHILLIP:
I'm Phillip Dimitrious. This is my daughter Miranda.
ARETHA:
I'm Aretha Tomalin. And this is Nino.
MIRANDA:
Tomlin? Like Lily Tomlin?

ARETHA:
No. Mine has an "A."
PHILLIP:
Who's Lily Tomlin?
ARETHA:
. . . The Aretha is because my mother is one of your very liberal socialist
types. We had a cleaning woman named . . .
MIRANDA:
. . . Aretha.
ARETHA:
. . . Who my mother loved, so she named me after her. (*To Phillip.*) Divorced?
PHILLIP:
Separated . . . How can you tell?
ARETHA:
It's on your face. Are you the famous architect, Phillip Dimitrious?
MIRANDA: (*Laughs.*)
He sure is.
ARETHA:
Let's grab a bite to eat and I'll tell you my life story.

CUT TO:

EXT. ATHENS CAFE—DAY

(*Aretha, Phillip and Miranda crossing busy square, go up steps to cafe, sit at table. During Aretha's speech, we notice a cute group of Greek teenage boys at a nearby table. One of the boys is flirting with Miranda.*)

ARETHA:
So . . . my first husband was an Israeli I met in the Museum of Modern Art in
New York. He dragged me back to Tel-Aviv. He was gorgeous. A Talmudic
scholar with two-foot eye lashes who taught swimming for a living. Which in
Israel is totally ridiculous, because Jews don't think they can float. Anyway,
he was crazy about his mother, and just maybe a little gay. In any case, that
didn't work out. Then I married a Greek psychiatrist in Jerusalem. He flew
me to Athens and we set up housekeeping. The problem was, I was his only
patient. The Greeks don't go much for head shrinking. Also, he took five hour
coffee breaks.

(*Waiter stops at table. Phillip orders.*)

PHILLIP: (*In Greek.*)
Two coffees . . . one coca-cola. Thank you.

ARETHA:
Anyhow, that didn't work either. So . . . that brings us up to the present. Do I talk a lot?
PHILLIP:
You. . . ?
ARETHA:
Oh, I can also sing "Hava Nagila" in two languages.

(*We see cute Greek boy flirt with Miranda. She notices and looks back.*)

MIRANDA:
I'm going to look for some music.

(*Miranda gets up and leaves. Cute Greek boy follows her.*)

ARETHA: (*Says to Phillip.*)
She's great . . . So that's how I work my way back . . . getting singing jobs.
PHILLIP:
Back to New York?
ARETHA:
Yeah . . . unless I fall in love with you. Which is a distinct possibility.
PHILLIP:
That would be a mistake. I'm right in the middle of a nervous breakdown.
ARETHA:
Who'd she run off with?
PHILLIP:
She didn't exactly run.
ARETHA:
You're in a lot of pain, eh?
PHILLIP:
So are you.
ARETHA:
Of course . . . Do you like me?
PHILLIP:
Hey . . . I like you.
ARETHA: (*Starts to get up.*)
Well anyway, I've got to go . . . wash my dog. Thanks for everything. (*She looks at him. Then she takes a key out of her purse and puts it on the table in front of Phillip.*) Look . . . I finish work at three. (*She indicates tag on key.*) This is my address . . . Come on, Nino. Say goodbye to the kid.

(*As Aretha leaves cafe, she bumps into Miranda who is on her way back to Phillip's table.*)

ARETHA:
Bye, Miranda. It was nice meeting you.
MIRANDA:
Bye. Bye, Nino.

(*Miranda returns to the table.*)

MIRANDA: (*To Phillip.*)
I like her. I like her a lot. But you better not do it.
PHILLIP:
You have no right to tell me what to do.
MIRANDA:
Why don't you send me to a private school . . . Pervert!

(*She rises to leave cafe. Phillip follows her as they exit cafe, run down stairs.*)

PHILLIP:
What did you call me? You're little, you're this big.
MIRANDA:
You're smaller.
PHILLIP:
You're a little shit-pot.

EXT. NIGHT PLAKA

(*Street is almost empty. Aretha walking down the street, humming a tune . . . Smiling to herself . . . As she passes a small cafe that is closing, she says goodnight to the owner, who waves back. Aretha enters her little garden.*)

INT. ARETHA'S APARTMENT

(*As she enters, Phillip sits on her bed, petting Nino.*)

PHILLIP:
Oh, hi . . . you worked late, huh?
ARETHA:
No. I told you I got off at three.
PHILLIP:
Listen, uh . . . uh . . .
ARETHA:
Aretha.
PHILLIP:
I know your name. Look, I'll be straight with you, Aretha. Oh, this is very

difficult for me . . .
ARETHA:
Going to bed with me is very difficult?
PHILLIP:
Not going to bed with you is very difficult . . . It's wrong. I can't do it. I came
to give you back your key in person. (*Hands her the key.*) You are one of the sex-
iest women I've ever seen. You're funny. You make me feel good. But it's
wrong.

(*Aretha has sat by now on the bed and is just staring at this amazing new encounter in her
life.*)

PHILLIP:
My daughter is only part of it. My life is very complicated right now. I have a
long list of reasons. Listen, five minutes after the sex, I'd be looking at my
watch, and I don't even have a watch . . . Not because the sex wasn't wonderful. Oh, the sex would be incredible. Of that I feel certain. It would be the
fourth of July! But . . . I'd be thinking about the kid, about my wife, waves,
storms, nightmares . . . electricals. You understand?
ARETHA:
Sure. Thanks for being honest.
PHILLIP:
You do understand, don't you?
ARETHA:
Yeah . . . (*Gets up from bed.*) The only reason I gave you my key is that I have
this terrible fear that the one who I should have given the key to and didn't is
the one that would have been perfect.

(*Aretha goes into the kitchen, Phillip follows.*)

PHILLIP:
There's no such thing as perfect.
ARETHA:
Not that I've given my key to that many men. I haven't. Really.

(*They smile.*)

PHILLIP:
I believe you.
ARETHA:
I've never been guilty about sex, so maybe I haven't been as selective as I
might have been. So . . . no more obligations.
PHILLIP:
Well . . . I tell you, I feel very relaxed.

ARETHA:
Would you like something to drink?
PHILLIP:
Okay . . . it's hot.
ARETHA:
How 'bout ice water.
PHILLIP:
I'd give a lot for a cold Sprite . . .

(*They exit apartment.*)

EXT. STREET—CAFE

ARETHA:
George, we need two cold Sprites, okay?
OWNER: (*He knows her.*)
Okay . . .

(*Aretha and Phillip sit down at a small table.*)

ARETHA:
So . . . okay . . . yeah . . . You were saying . . . about your storms and electrical appliances?
PHILLIP:
What?

(*The owner brings the Sprites.*)

ARETHA:
Your dreams, nightmares?

(*Phillip gets up, leans over and kisses Aretha—bringing her to her feet. They embrace. It's hot. They turn and walk back to Aretha's apartment. Phillip tries to pay owner.*)

PHILLIP:
George, we pay after, eh?

DISSOLVE TO:

INT. NIGHTCLUB—ATHENS—NIGHT

(*Aretha is on stage singing "Hava Nagila." Phillip stands at the bar, watching her. Lots of Japanese tourists, taking flash pictures. A table of stony-faced Arabs. Aretha finishes, there is applause.*)

ARETHA:
Thank you . . . Thank you very much. Are there any requests?

(*Enter Alonzo and Antonia. Accompanied by Harry, Sebastian and Trinc.*)

ALONZO:
"Volare."

(*Phillip turns to see who the voice belongs to.*)

ARETHA:
Volare? That went out with what's his name.
ALONZO:
Sing it, please.

WIDE ANGLE

(*As Aretha goes into "Volare," the entourage sits at a table. Phillip walks over to them and joins them. He is surprised and angry. Antonia is happy to see him.*)

PHILLIP:
Well . . . this is *not* a nice surprise.
ALONZO:
Be nice . . we come as friends.
ANTONIA:
Hello, Phillip.
PHILLIP:
Same old gang.
ANTONIA:
Where's Miranda?
PHILLIP:
Sleeping. How did you find me? How did you know I was here?
ALONZO:
We know everything. Including the singer.
ANTONIA: (*To Alonzo.*)
Don't.

(*Alonzo is quiet.*)

ANTONIA:
We have to talk, Phillip.
PHILLIP:
He listens to you. You must be satisfying him.

ALONZO:
Still a boy . . . a boy.

ANTONIA:
I want to take Miranda home with me.

PHILLIP:
Home? Where is home?

ANTONIA:
The apartment.

PHILLIP:
Does he stay there, too?

ALONZO:
I spend time there. Phillip, I am honest with you. I love Antonia. I want her to be happy. She wants her child back.

ANTONIA:
Summer is over, Phillip.

PHILLIP:
Why don't we let Miranda decide what she wants?

(*Aretha's number ends. They all applaud. Aretha joins them at the table. The Greek M.C. announces a belly dancer who replaces Aretha on the stage.*)

ARETHA:
Hi . . . I'm Aretha Tomalin. I'm the new girl.

PHILLIP:
This is Aretha Tomalin . . . the new girl . . .

ARETHA: (*To Alonzo.*)
And you must be the new guy . . . and the doctor, the lawyer, and the comic.

ALONZO: (*Laughs.*)
Anytime you are looking for a new job, call me, Miss Tomalin, I can always use a fortune teller.

ARETHA:
That's what they all say.

ANTONIA:
Phillip, we made a deal. Summer's over, I want her back . . . she's my child. I'm not going to fool around about this!

PHILLIP:
We can talk about it tomorrow.

(*He turns to go.*)

ARETHA: (*To Antonia.*)
You remind me a lot of Miranda.

ANTONIA:
Thank you . . . I like the way you sing.

ARETHA:
Oh, thank you. I like the way you look.
PHILLIP:
I like the way I feel.
ALONZO:
Don't run out on us, Phillip.
PHILLIP:
Or else? What?
ALONZO:
Listen . . . I haven't had a cold in two months. I sleep like a baby. My blood pressure is one-thirty over . . .
SEBASTIAN:
Eighty-five.
ALONZO:
Eighty-five. All because Antonia makes me happy. So, please. You make her happy, too.
PHILLIP: (*Angry.*)
I don't like threats!
ALONZO:
Threats? Those weren't threats. You'll know when I threaten you.
ARETHA:
Well, it was really nice meeting you all. Ciao, Ciao . . .

(*Phillip and Aretha exit. By now Trinc is up on the stage with the belly dancer. Alonzo takes Antonia's hand affectionately . . . She is quite upset.*)

EXT. ROOFTOP—ATHENS—DAWN

(*T.V. aerials blur the view of the Acropolis, but it is still a powerful image. Phillip is at his telescope. Aretha still in her nightclub outfit, stands with him. Miranda, in her night-gown, comes out on the rooftop and walks over to them.*)

MIRANDA: (*To Phillip.*)
I hate you.
PHILLIP:
Tough.
MIRANDA:
I'm not going back.
PHILLIP:
Yes, you are.
ARETHA:
. . . I know the islands.
MIRANDA:
What islands?

PHILLIP: (*To Aretha.*)
This is not your problem. You stay out of this.
ARETHA:
How could you say that to me . . .
PHILLIP:
I don't want any more commitments.
ARETHA:
Who the hell is asking for a commitment?
PHILLIP:
This is not the time for semantics. There are commitments and there are commitments.
MIRANDA: (*To Aretha.*)
What island?
ARETHA:
There are a lot of islands. If we chose one . . . nobody would ever find us.
MIRANDA:
I want to go.
PHILLIP:
What about your mother?
MIRANDA:
What about her?
PHILLIP:
What about school?
MIRANDA:
You could teach me.
PHILLIP:
What about your mother? Don't you want to see your mother?
MIRANDA:
As long as she's with that guy, I don't want to see her.
PHILLIP:
Are you sure, kid?
MIRANDA:
Yeah . . . Please.
PHILLIP: (*To Aretha.*)
Are you sure?
ARETHA: (*To Phillip.*)
Are you sure?
PHILLIP:
Yes, I'm sure.
ARETHA:
I'm sure.

(*Phillip hugs Miranda, then pulls Aretha in too.*)

EXT. SEA AND ISLAND—DAY

(*A rugged, bare-chested Greek boatsman, Vassili, holds the tiller of an old fishing boat. Phillip, Miranda, Aretha and Nino sit amidst cartons and crates filled with vegetables, fruit, etc. Phillip's telescope, carefully wrapped, sticks out between two of their suitcases. An old lady in black sits on a crate, eating grapes.*)

FULL SHOT OF COVE AND VILLAGE

(*Mostly abandoned houses clinging to the steep hills. A white pebble beach. It is beautiful. The boat moves toward the shore.*)

ANGLE ON BOAT

ARETHA:
Is beautiful, eh?
PHILLIP:
It's paradise! (*Points to tower.*) That's where we'll live.
ARETHA:
Allright!
MIRANDA:
That'll be my room.
PHILLIP:
Yeah . . . Vassili. Where are all the people?
VASSILI:
Not many people here. Everybody go to Australia, Germany, Mexico . . . look for jobs, work . . .
PHILLIP:
What about the women . . . children . . .
VASSILI:
No . . . no women, children. Only goats, sheep.

(*They all look up as a voice calls from the cliffs above. ANGLE ON HIGH HILLSIDE. Figure of Kalibanos is seen jumping up and down. Several goats are with him.*)

KALIBANOS:
Hey, Yasoo. Welcome. I am Kalibanos. I am Kalibanos.
PHILLIP: (*Calls.*)
I am Phillip . . . I am Phillip. (*To Vassili.*) Who is that?
VASSILI:
Kalibanos . . . He crazy. Sleep with goats . . .
PHILLIP: (*Laughs.*)
He sleeps with goats!

ANGLE ON WHITE ROCK BEACH

(*Kalibanos is running down from the cliff onto the beach, calling out to the boat.*)

KALIBANOS:
Hey . . . Hey . . . I am big guy on island. I am the boss. I also guide. I show you dirty statues in cave.

(*He stops at donkey standing on the beach, and pulls a uniform coat and hat out of the saddle bag. He changes into them as he keeps up his spiel.*)

ANGLE ON BOAT

ARETHA:
We're looking for a condominium with a southern exposure!
KALIBANOS:
Yes . . . (*To donkey.*) What is condominium?

(*He continues to run toward the dock, trying to arrive in time to meet the boat.*)

EXT. DOCK—DAY

(*As the boat arrives, the young boy/boat-hand jumps off and secures the ropes. Phillip, Aretha, and Miranda get off, and the boy starts handing down their suitcases. Kalibanos arrives just in time, and catches the dog as Phillip throws it to him.*)

PHILLIP:
This is Nino.
KALIBANOS:
Welcome, Phillip.
PHILLIP:
Kalibanos, eh?
MIRANDA: (*As she gets off boat.*)
Hi.
KALIBANOS:
Name?
MIRANDA:
Miranda. (*They shake hands.*)
KALIBANOS:
Welcome. (*Aretha gets off boat.*) Name?
ARETHA:
Aretha. (*She salutes him.*)
KALIBANOS:
Welcome, Aretha. Hey, Phillip—you got a cigarette?

(*Phillip tosses him a pack.*)

PHILLIP:
Keep the pack.
KALIBANOS:
Efcharisto. Hey, Aretha . . How much for sunglasses?
ARETHA:
Be my guest. (*She tosses him the glasses.*)
KALIBANOS:
Oh, thank you . . . Kalibanos, fancy guy, eh?

(*He postures with cigarette and glasses. Vassili calls out to Kalibanos in Greek and a heated exchange follows.*)

MIRANDA:
What are they saying?
PHILLIP:
He doesn't understand why I have two women and he doesn't have any . . .

(*Miranda watches a little brown goat pick her way toward the dock.*)

MIRANDA:
Cute goat!
KALIBANOS:
Ah, that's my sweet Beatrice. (*He turns back to Phillip, and picks up the telescope admiringly.*)
PHILLIP:
Can I have that please—it's very delicate.

(*Kalibanos hands telescope to Phillip.*)

PHILLIP:
Could you get these suitcases, please?
KALIBANOS: (*Pause.*)
Okay, boss.

(*Vassili calls to Phillip from the boat.*)

VASSILI:
I come once a month. You raise flag, you want me.
PHILLIP:
I raise the flag if I want you to stop, right? Thank you. Bye!

(*Vassili waves as the boat backs away from the dock. Aretha looks after it, lost in thought*

. . . we end the flashback and . . .

CUT TO:

(Aretha's face as she drops rug . . .)

PULL BACK

(Miranda and Aretha drop the rug into the water. We're back in the cove.)

ARETHA:
Just don't fall for an architect who's into celibacy. *(Shouts up to the stone cottage.)* I'm tired of being a prisoner! *(To Miranda.)* Did you ever think of our typical day? What do we do? Sweep the floor . . . bake the bread, feed the chickens, feed the goats . . .

MIRANDA:
Wash the clothes, clean the rug, press the olives . . .

ARETHA:
Press the grapes.

MIRANDA: *(Shouts up to cottage.)*
Build the theatre!

ARETHA: *(Shouts.)*
Wash the windows! I don't do windows!

(We see Phillip step out onto the terrace, with Nino under his arm.)

PHILLIP: *(Shouts to them.)*
We're trying to take a nap.

ARETHA & MIRANDA:
We're tired of being prisoners!

PHILLIP:
Tough shit.

(Aretha and Miranda wag their fingers at him. Phillip looks down. Smiles.)

ARETHA & MIRANDA:
Ooouuuh! . . .

(It reminds them of a song, and they go into a harmonizing routine of "Why Do Fools Fall in Love," complete with gestures. Phillip watches from above, laughs.)

ANGLE ON COVE

(Aretha and Miranda are hysterical at their own performance. They fall into the water,

splashing and swimming and singing.)

CUT TO:

EXT./INT. HOUSE—ISLAND—SIESTA TIME—DAY

(*It is the middle of the day, and people, animals and nature are all settling down for their siesta . . . A great tree sighs and rests its branches. Nino falls asleep on his master's chair. The donkey falls asleep on the white-rocked beach. The chickens sleep on the tree's branches. Mary, the pet goat, falls asleep under the olive trees. The banners on top of the house settle down. The water in the cove is still . . . Aretha sleeps in the hammock under the trees by the cove.*)

CUT TO:

EXT. OLIVE TREES: TANGO MUSIC IS HEARD

(*CAMERA PANS across the cove to Phillip's house. Phillip steps onto the terrace and stops in the archway at the top of the outside stairs. He hears music as he looks around the cove. It seems to be coming from a deserted tower opposite the house.*)

ANGLE ON TOWER

(*We see Miranda, wearing Aretha's nightclub gown and lots of makeup. She dances a sexy tango, pretending she has a partner.*)

ANGLE ON PHILLIP

(*Confused.*)

HIS POV

(*Miranda dancing the tango, appears and disappears behind the stone walls. Phillip doesn't recognize her for a moment . . . Then he sees Antonia dance the tango, wearing the same dress as Miranda. Phillip races down the stairs, and up the narrow path leading to Miranda's tower.*)

ANGLE ON TOWER

(*As Phillip comes rushing through doorway, Miranda spots Phillip. She is embarrassed and quickly stops dancing. She turns the music off.*)

PHILLIP:
I thought you were your mother.

MIRANDA:
Mom is beautiful. I'm ugly.
PHILLIP:
You're beautiful. You wear too much makeup, but you ain't ugly kiddo.
MIRANDA:
Please . . . don't call me kiddo.
PHILLIP: (*As he turns music back on.*)
Dance with me?
MIRANDA:
No . . . cut it out . . . stop it please . . .
PHILLIP:
I need you to dance with me. We have no contact . . .

(*He reaches for Miranda but she shoves him away. They struggle.*)

MIRANDA:
No, stop it please. Leave me alone!
PHILLIP: (*Sits on ledge.*)
Why are you angry with me?
MIRANDA:
I hate it here! I'm bored! I can't stand you. You're crazy.

(*Miranda has been packing up the make-up, mirror and her bag—she picks up tape recorder. She is trying to keep from breaking into tears, and is edging toward the tower entrance.*)

PHILLIP:
This is paradise here. You're learning things here you'd never get a chance to do.
MIRANDA:
Can I be honest with you?
PHILLIP:
Yes.
MIRANDA:
You have a severe case of "folie a deux"!

(*Miranda picks up everything and exits. She's close to tears. Phillip is baffled.*)

EXT. AMPHITHEATRE—DAY

(*Kalibanos sits with Beatrice.*)

KALIBANOS:
You hungry, huh? You always eat . . . What you thinking, Beatrice?

(*He pats Beatrice and she baas to him.*)

KALIBANOS:
You think of love? Who do you like best? You love other goat or you love Kalibanos? You like Kalibanos? Sweet Beatrice wants music, eh?

(*Kalibanos picks up his clarinet and plays a beautiful Greek melody. The other goats, grazing on the slopes of the theatre, hear the music too. They all start moving towards the stage and mill around as Kalibanos now is singing to them. Kalibanos stands and starts playing "New York, New York."*)

MUSIC: "NEW YORK, NEW YORK"

(*The goats react by lining up, and Beatrice prances along in front of the line. Kalibanos puts his clarinet down and picks up his shepherd's cane. He dances down the steps and joins his goats on the stage. They are lined up like a chorus line and Kalibanos struts his stuff in front of them. The goats react by jumping up and down to the rhythm of the tune, like a chorus line. Finally, Kalibanos struts back up the steps and finishes the tune. The goats and Kalibanos all exit through the archway of the amphitheatre.*)

DISSOLVE TO:

EXT.—DAY

(*Phillip and Aretha lying together in the hammock. Aretha lies on top of Phillip.*)

PHILLIP:
. . . Just not in the mood for love.
ARETHA:
Phil, I don't get it—I mean this is getting too complicated even for me. Neurotic is a word I always related to . . . But now we're dealing with crazy.
PHILLIP:
Aretha.
ARETHA:
Yeah?
PHILLIP:
Have you had a good time so far? Have you had an interesting time?
ARETHA:
So far was a long time ago. What started out as an adventure has turned into a life sentence!
PHILLIP:
I dunno . . . I'm a little worried about my theatre.
ARETHA:
Why? Are you afraid Euripides will finish his new play, and you won't be

ready?

PHILLIP:

I'm afraid I don't have the smart words anymore. But I like it. I just like it.

ARETHA:

Can I have a hug?

PHILLIP: (*Gives her a hug.*)

Oooh, you're so Greek.

ARETHA:

Maybe you're right. Maybe the sex is not what it's all about. Maybe even if I *was* getting it regular as my friend Phyllis used to say, I still wouldn't be happy. Maybe what I really want is a regular guy and a baby . . .

PHILLIP:

Ouch . . .

ARETHA:

. . . And a house in the suburbs and a manicure once a week . . .

PHILLIP:

Ouch! . . . You have the humor girl. You really have the humor.

ARETHA:

It's running out fast . . . you know what I mean.

PHILLIP:

I may stay here forever.

ARETHA:

Phil, it's getting kind of sick for the kid.

(*He looks at her.*)

ARETHA:

Today Kalibanos made a pass at her. He kissed her.

(*Phillip leaps up, possessed, angry. He smacks the hanging bells, causing them to* RING OUT.)

EXT. AMPHITHEATRE—DAY

(*Kalibanos is taking a nap with Beatrice. He wakes up with a start. Kalibanos hears the bells. He is frightened.*)

EXT. HILLSIDE BELOW HOUSE—DAY

(*Phillip running, chased by the dog.*)

EXT. PATH

(*Kalibanos running.*)

KALIBANOS:
Bad bongolongo bells! Phillip is angry!

ANGLE ON KALIBANOS

(*Terror* . . . *CAMERA TRACKING CLOSER AND CLOSER TO his face as he runs.*)

CUT TO:

FLASHBACK

(*Phillip is sitting at the table, pointing to various pictures on a large chart he has drawn. Kalibanos is leaning over him, trying to read the names. Phillip points to "octopus" as Kalibanos tries to spell it.*

Kalibanos is sitting in the cave, at a simple but efficient combing machine, through which he pulls strands of sheep's wool as Phillip watches.

Phillip is standing in the field next to the cave, pitching a baseball to Kalibanos, who is desperately trying to hit the ball. He finally does.

Kalibanos plays the clarinet. Phillip dances a step that Kalibanos has taught him.)

END FLASHBACK

ANGLE ON KALIBANOS—RUNNING

EXT. DOCK AND SEA (ISLAND)

(*Kalibanos running towards small fishing boat. Phillip and dog running to the boat, too. Phillip throws the dog at Kalibanos and gets in the boat.*)

ANGLE ON BOAT

(*As Kalibanos jumps in. Phillip holds Nino.*)

PHILLIP:
Row . . . Row . . .
KALIBANOS: (*Rowing.*)
Son-of-a-bitch storm coming, Boss.
PHILLIP:
Is that what you're worried about?
KALIBANOS:
Yes, sir.

PHILLIP:
Looks like a beautiful day to me. What do you think, Dog?

(*They are approaching the mouth of the cove.*)

KALIBANOS:
Dog not know shit about weather.
PHILLIP:
Remember I taught you not to lie?
KALIBANOS:
I don't lie.
PHILLIP:
That's very good . . . What did you do to Miranda this morning?
KALIBANOS:
I watch her swim . . .
PHILLIP:
Later, I mean later . . .
KALIBANOS:
Okay, okay . . . I look at her melones.
PHILLIP:
Then what?
KALIBANOS:
Okay. I show her my T.V.
PHILLIP:
Your what?
KALIBANOS:
Sony Color Control Trinitron . . . 12 inches . . . Is wonderful . . .
PHILLIP:
Did you touch her?
KALIBANOS:
No, sir.
PHILLIP: (*Wild.*)
Lies!
KALIBANOS:
I hold her hand. Like friend. Hello, Miranda. Hello.
PHILLIP:
Then what?

(*Phillip motions to Kalibanos to stand up in the boat.*)

KALIBANOS: (*Sees the anger, can't lie.*)
Okay. I kissed her. It was beautiful.

(*Phillip hits Kalibanos with the oar, sending him into the sea. Phillip keeps hitting Kali-*

banos in the water with the oar every time he gets close to the boat.)

KALIBANOS:
Help, help.
PHILLIP:
She was my baby!
KALIBANOS:
No baby . . She is woman. Look for yourself.
PHILLIP:
I was your friend. I helped you.
KALIBANOS:
I was boss before you showed up!
PHILLIP:
You were ignorant and superstitious. I taught you to read and write and fix
the pump and read the stars.
KALIBANOS: (*Gasping.*)
I show you the olive and the figs and sweet water. I give you my back and now
you drown me because my bonijoni dance in my pants.
PHILLIP:
She is my baby!
KALIBANOS: (*Starting to go under.*)
Soon she want the bonijoni in her. Soon she dance in the night for amore, for
love . . . With who? You? Only me. Only Kalibanos!

(*Phillip throws the oar at Kalibanos. He goes under, but this time doesn't come up . . .
Phillip leaps into the sea.*)

EXT. SEA—UNDERWATER SHOT

(*Phillip finds Kalibanos and helps him rise to the surface.*)

EXT. SEA SURFACE

(*As they pop up, Kalibanos gasping for breath . . . Phillip hauls him back towards the
boat.*)

KALIBANOS:
You God, Boss . . .
PHILLIP:
I'm no God. I'm a monkey, just like you.

(*SOUND OF A BOAT HORN IS HEARD. They both turn. Way in the distance, we see a
yacht.*)

EXT. YACHT—DAY

(*A magnificent ship. Freddie Alonzo is looking through binoculars on front deck. Trinc is on the deck with Freddie, working out on an exercycle, smoking a cigar.*)

TRINC:
This is the life . . . isn't this terrific? Know what I gave up for this? Nothing. I think when I die, I'll come back as myself.
FREDDIE:
A couple of natives are taking a dip . . .
TRINC:
Smell that air . . . Pittsburgh.
FREDDIE:
Wish there was some surf.
TRINC:
You'd only get bored . . . Surfboard . . .
FREDDIE:
Pretty corny, Mr. Trinc.
TRINC:
Bet your old man laughs at it.
FREDDIE:
Okay . . . a hundred drachmas.
TRINC:
You're on!

EXT. STERN DECK—ANGLE ON DECK CHAIRS

(*Dolores is sitting draped over a rattan chair, singing and playing a small harp. She is a gorgeous blonde. Harry and Antonia are lounging nearby. Antonia is reading.*)

DOLORES: (*Stops playing.*)
I look around at the sea and I wonder . . . "What is man's destiny?" It's all a deep mystery, deep and dark, like the sea . . . How sad.
ANTONIA:
Those are pretty deep thoughts. What time is it Harry?
HARRY:
My stomach tells me it's time for lunch.
ANTONIA:
I hope Alonzo is better . . . He had a rotten night.
HARRY:
Sorry . . . How are you?
ANTONIA:
Strange, as usual.

HARRY:
Strange is better than middling.
ANTONIA:
I just can't figure out what I'm doing here.
DOLORES:
You know, Antonia, you gotta try to enjoy yourself. Go with the moment.
ANTONIA:
You know, I tried that one . . . I just can't get it to work for me.
DOLORES:
It didn't work for me either. Until Gurdjieff.
ANTONIA:
Gurdjieff?
DOLORES:
You know Gurdjieff, don't you?
ANTONIA:
Intimately . . . let's get some lunch.

(*Antonia gets up . . . kisses Dolores on the forehead, and all three go downstairs to the main deck.*)

EXT./INT. YACHT—ANGLE MAIN DECK CABIN

(*Dr. Sebastian, looking very natty in a trendy boat outfit, is pushing Alonzo in a wheelchair.*)

SEBASTIAN:
You shouldn't just sit. You should be walking.
ALONZO:
My feet hurt. You're my doctor, not my nurse.
SEBASTIAN:
Sometimes I wish it was the other way around.

(*The wheelchair comes into view on the deck.*)

ANTONIA:
Good morning. How do you feel?

(*Two sailors help Alonzo into a chair opposite Antonia at the breakfast table. All the others sit around.*)

ALONZO:
How do I feel? I got a knife in my colon. My head feels like a brain tumor. Planter's warts on both feet and I haven't taken a good crap in a week. Other than that, I'm perfect.

(Antonia gets up, angry, and leaves the table. Alonzo gets up and follows her.)

ANGLE ON ANTONIA AND ALONZO ON THE SIDE OF THE DECK

ALONZO:
Sorry. Forgive me, Antonia.
ANTONIA:
Look . . . I'm not part of your entourage . . . If you're sick, I'm sorry. But don't ever talk to me like that.
ALONZO:
Please, be happy . . .
ANTONIA:
Maybe we've just come to the end.
ALONZO:
You and me?
ANTONIA:
No. The trip . . . Yes . . . Everything. I don't know. It's me. I'm hopeless. I don't know what I'm doing anymore . . .
ALONZO:
This is Freddie's holiday.
ANTONIA:
I'm right on the edge, Alonzo.
ALONZO: *(Takes her hand.)*
A new leaf. Starting now, okay?

(They stroll back to the table.)

ANGLE ON TABLE

FREDDIE:
I like New York.
DOLORES:
I like L.A. so much better . . . You're more in touch with your body.
SEBASTIAN:
I prefer the new bi-coastiality . . . Brighton Beach and Venice!
FREDDIE:
Are you all right, Dad?
ALONZO:
Yeah . . . Wonderful. I feel like a million dollars.
TRINC:
Ah, but that's peanuts to you. Hey did you hear about the kid who wanted to surf? But there's no waves. So this other kid tells him he's bored. He's surf-board.

(Alonzo roars with laughter. He is the only one to laugh, of course. Freddie hands a dollar to Trinc.)

FREDDIE:
You win Mr. Trinc.

(He goes around the table.)

ALONZO:
Where you going?
FREDDIE:
I'm going to do some scuba diving.
ALONZO:
Be careful. The water is tricky in these islands.

(A sudden breeze stirs the ship . . . Trinc's hat flies off and blows into the water. Trinc jumps up dramatically.)

TRINC:
Hat overboard!

ANGLE ON TRINC'S CAP IN THE WATER

(Water is a bit choppy.)

EXT. SEA—UNDERWATER SHOT

(Miranda swimming . . . we see a figure coming towards her. She sees the figure. It comes closer. It is Freddie, wearing scuba gear. They come close to each other. They stare. They surface.)

EXT. MIRANDA'S COVE

(As they pop up. Miranda is frightened for a moment. Freddie takes his mask off. He just stares at her. She is speechless.)

FREDDIE:
. . . Me Freddie.
MIRANDA: *(Pretending.)*
. . . Me Miranda.
FREDDIE:
Me, from boat.
MIRANDA:
Me, from island.

(She gestures towards the shore.)

FREDDIE:
You speak good English.
MIRANDA:
Me learn from tourists.

(They swim towards shore.)

FREDDIE:
Me . . . I'm seventeen years old. You?
MIRANDA:
Fifteen years.

(She steps onto the rocks.)

FREDDIE:
You're beautiful.
MIRANDA:
Me ugly.

(Freddie laughs.)

FREDDIE:
No way. You're real neat.

(Now they sit on the rocks. He takes his equipment off. Miranda puts her hand to her heart to feel it. It is pounding.)

FREDDIE:
You okay?
MIRANDA:
Oh, yeah. Me okay.

(She gets up.)

MIRANDA:
Freddie, come see other side. Is beautiful . . .

(Freddie follows her up the cliff. They come over the crest and climb down to the next cove. The view is spectacular.)

FREDDIE:
Boy, what I wouldn't give for a slice of New York pizza right now . . .

MIRANDA:
With a root-beer float.
FREDDIE:
Are you putting me on?
MIRANDA:
Yeah. I'm American.
FREDDIE:
What are you doing here?
MIRANDA:
I live here.
FREDDIE:
Oh . . . You into some kind of commune?
MIRANDA:
It's a long story . . . Is punk still big in the States?
FREDDIE:
No, Pop . . .
MIRANDA:
How's it go?
FREDDIE:
Something like this.

(*They stroll along the water's edge.*)

CUT TO:

EXT. YACHT

(*A launch is leaving the yacht. Two sailors in the launch, along with Antonia, Alonzo, Harry, Dolores, Sebastian and Trinc. Picnic baskets, champagne. Alonzo calls out to his secretary.*)

ALONZO:
Stella, if there are any phone calls for me . . . Tell them I don't want to be disturbed. I'm busy!
SECRETARY: (*In the yacht.*)
Okay, Mr. Alonzo!
ALONZO: (*To Antonia.*)
Today I swim. We surprise Freddie.
TRINC:
Hey Alonzo, I talked to the Doc . . . Your health is great. He's touching up your X-rays.

(*Alonzo laughs.*)

DOLORES: (*Smiles, she likes Trinc.*)
Oh Arnie, that's the oldest joke in the world.
TRINC:
I think I stole it from myself.
ALONZO: (*To Antonia.*)
It's a beautiful island, isn't it.
ANTONIA:
It's beautiful. Like a dream.
ALONZO:
There used to be pirates here—strange and powerful warriors.
ANTONIA:
Like you?
ALONZO:
Have I lost you?

(*At this moment the boat rocks back and forth. Trinc grabs hat. Sebastian turns pale.*)

SEBASTIAN:
It's getting rough.
SAILOR:
It is a bit choppy, Mr. Alonzo. Il mare e molto mosso.
ALONZO:
Avanti! Coraggio! Siamo tutti pirati!

EXT. COVE & PEBBLE BEACH—DAY

(*Kalibanos running toward Phillip's house.*)

EXT. HOUSE—DAY

(*Aretha is sitting in the kitchen doorway, reading, when Kalibanos comes running up the steps.*)

KALIBANOS:
Aretha! Where is Phil?

(*Aretha simply points up.*)

INT. BEDROOM—DAY

(*Phillip is sitting at his desk, studying a baseball book and talking to the dog, Nino, who is sitting on the window sill behind him. Kalibanos rushes in.*)

PHILLIP:

I don't think they'll ever break Joe DiMaggio's record! 56 straight games in 1941 . . . Better than Roger Maris, Babe Ruth . . . Do you understand? A baseball player . . .

KALIBANOS: (*Trying to get Phillip's attention.*)

Phil . . . Phil . . . Phil . . . Tourist boat is coming . . . Phil . . . Tourist boat—a hundred tourist in one boat. Coming to island . . . Look . . . we can sell them the starfish, lots of coca-cola, the eight foot octopipi leg . . . Listen . . . come . . . Look . . . look! Tourist come in boat to island!

(*Kalibanos pulls Phillip to the window overlooking the sea. Phillip looks out, but is really not very interested.*)

PHILLIP:
Great. Great . . . That's great.

(*Phillip returns to his book. Kalibanos is desperate.*)

KALIBANOS:
Please, boss, make tourists stop here. Chance to make big money, sell T.V., Gucci loafers . . .
PHILLIP:
Stop shouting!
KALIBANOS:
Come . . . I show you in telescope!

(*He runs out on the terrace.*)

PHILLIP:
Hey, you leave my telescope alone . . .

(*Phillip follows him onto the terrace.*)

EXT. TERRACE—DAY

(*Phillip grabs the telescope before Kalibanos can get it. He carries it to the edge of the terrace overlooking the sea, and sets it up. Kalibanos keeps pointing and shouting. Then a moment of silence while Phillip looks through the scope.*)

EXT. SEA—DAY

(*POV of the launch approaching. Its cargo is now clearly visible: Sebastian, Trinc, Harry, Dolores, Alonzo . . . Antonia!*)

ANGLE ON PHILLIP AND KALIBANOS

(*Phillip takes his eye from the eyepiece. He is strangely calm.*)

PHILLIP:
They found us.
KALIBANOS:
Who found us?
PHILLIP:
They found us.
KALIBANOS:
You mean tourists find us.
PHILLIP:
They found us.
KALIBANOS:
Okay . . . Okay . . . They found us.

(*He goes toward the outside steps to tell Aretha. Phillip looks up at the sky.*)

PHILLIP: (*Raises his eyeglasses to the sky like a prism.*)
Show me the magic.

(*The wind and the sky seem to respond. The water in the cove ripples.*)

PHILLIP:
Show me the magic!!

EXT. SKY—DAY

(*Blackish clouds appear. Phillip's umbrella, still set up on his tower, is blown over by the wind. Chickens are blown across the white rocks. The pet goat, Mary, is pushed by the wind.*)

EXT. HOUSE—DAY

(*Kalibanos runs toward the kitchen door to find Aretha. The wind is whistling now. They both have to shout.*)

KALIBANOS:
They found us!
ARETHA:
Who found us?
KALIBANOS:
Tourist boat found us . . . Come on, I show you!

(*They both run up the outside steps leading up to the terrace.*)

EXT. SKY—DAY

(*Dark, ominous clouds are forming. [This scene is the first Special Effects Matte Shot.]
The bells on the terrace are shaken by the wind. The banners on top of the house flap wildly
and fly off. The solar unit on top of the house shakes, finally breaks and falls off.*)

TERRACE

(*Phillip, pleased with his "magic," wipes his eye-glasses on the hem of his robe. Now he
begins to jump up and down, almost an incantation to the gods. The storm increases in in-
tensity as Phillip dances around the terrace. Kalibanos and Aretha run onto the terrace. She
is frightened by Phillip's strange dancing. Kalibanos leads her to the telescope and shows
her the launch. Phillip suddenly races into the house.*)

PHILLIP:
They want a storm, I'll give them a storm.

INT. HOUSE

(*Phillip closes the shutters. The wild wind smashes the lanterns to the floor. Phillip goes
down and closes the rear patio doors. The storm is getting wilder.*)

EXT. HOUSE

(*Phillip comes out. Using his hand as a "magic wand," he gestures towards the heavens.
Now the sky becomes unbelievably intense. Purple—black clouds—thunder—lightning.*)

EXT. STAIRS TO TERRACE—DAY

(*As Phillip comes bounding up the stairs, Kalibanos meets him.*)

KALIBANOS: (*Frightened.*)
You God, Boss . . .

(*Phillip runs past him, onto the terrace.*)

EXT. TERRACE—DAY

(*Phillip runs to the telescope to see how his victims are doing. Aretha tries to hold him
back.*)

EXT. LAUNCH—RAIN

(*Big wave tosses the boat high in the air. The basket of champagne goes overboard. The group is frightened.*)

ALONZO:
Get us back to the yacht!
SAILOR:
We're better off making for shore, sir . . . Life jackets everybody.
ALONZO:
Get us in then.

(*Everyone is putting on life jackets.*)

DOLORES:
Oh God . . . Is this our destiny? To be drowned in a magic storm?

EXT. ISLAND

(*Freddie and Miranda running along the shore. Rain is pouring down. Sky is black.*)

EXT. TERRACE

(*Phillip is dancing in the rain. Dog is wild. Kalibanos and Aretha are at the telescope.*)

PHILLIP:
They wanted a storm. I'll give them a storm.
ARETHA:
You've got to stop this!
KALIBANOS:
Boss made storm!

(*As if in immediate response, the wind blows Phillip around, bells fly loose.*)

PHILLIP: (*To the heavens.*)
Stop it! Okay, stop it!

(*The telescope is torn free by the wind and falls down.*)

PHILLIP:
Stop it, I said!

(*Now the awning overhead crashes down on Phillip, Kalibanos and Aretha. Even Phillip is frightened. Dog wails.*)

PHILLIP:
Miranda . . . ?

KALIBANOS:
Boss no God. Only God God.

(*Phillip and Aretha run down the stairs.*)

EXT. LAUNCH

(*Trinc is sitting on the gunnel of the boat. He is blown overboard.*)

ANGLE ON WATER

(*Trinc waving desperately.*)

SEBASTIAN:
Trinc . . . Trinc . . .

(*Sebastian leaps in to save Trinc, holding onto his toupee.*)

EXT. PEBBLE BEACH—RAIN

(*Kalibanos running . . . He spots some debris from the launch. Two bottles of champagne and a jar of Noxema and Harry's wet Stetson. He scoops them up and runs.*)

EXT. LAUNCH

(*Capsizes. All overboard.*)

EXT. SEA

(*Sailor swimming for Harry. Harry gets swept away.*)

EXT. ROCKY SHORE—DAY

(*Phillip and Aretha running. He stops. Sees something. Nino runs ahead. Miranda and Freddie are standing on the beach in the pouring rain. Phillip and Aretha join Miranda and Freddie.*)

PHILLIP:
Where the hell did he come from?
MIRANDA:
The boat . . . Dad, this is Freddie . . .

(*Suddenly, miraculously, there is a change of light. The rain stops. Phillip looks at the sky. Freddie and Miranda look out at the sea, then run towards it. Aretha follows them.*)

EXT. ISLAND—DAY

(*The sky is clear, the rain has stopped. Magically, the clouds disappear, and the sun is seen. Phillip runs towards the sea. Nino chases after him.*)

EXT. SEA

(*We see Aretha swimming towards Alonzo to rescue him. Phillip swims for Antonia. The sea is calming down now. ANGLE ON ANTONIA who sees Phillip. She can't believe it. ANGLE ON PHILLIP AND ANTONIA as he reaches her. Miranda and Freddie reach Dolores and swim her toward the shore.*)

DOLORES: (*Holding her harp.*)
. . . It's a miracle . . . I'm going to write a book about it.

(*Aretha reaches Alonzo and helps him onto the shore.*)

INT. CAVE

(*Kalibanos sitting in his bed . . . drinking champagne . . . goats baaing . . . Kalibanos puts down champagne and opens the jar of Noxzema. Sniffs at it. The booze and the smell are getting him high. He dips a finger into the jar and comes up with a scoop. He sniffs it, then slowly, licks it. He swallows . . . his mouth begins to burn. He pants wildly . . . He suddenly reacts to noises at the entrance of the cave.*)

ANGLE ON MOUTH OF CAVE

(*Sebastian and Trinc enter, soaked . . . disoriented.*)

TRINC: (*Looks around.*)
Talk about urban renewal.

(*Sebastian's toupee is half off. He wrings the water out of it.*)

SEBASTIAN:
They said you could swim in it.

(*Kalibanos, terrified, puts a huge octopus skin over his head and hides. He pants loudly, the Noxzema now foaming over his lips.*)

TRINC:
Smells like something in heat.
SEBASTIAN:
Could be a vampire bat.

TRINC: (*Sees Kalibanos.*)
It's a fish in drag.

(*Kalibanos pants wildly as he steps out to face them, the octopus skin still on his head. Trinc and Sebastian recoil in horror.*)

TRINC:
Smells like a cough-drop factory.
SEBASTIAN:
I think he's a bandido.

(*Kalibanos throws off the skin and reveals himself proudly.*)

KALIBANOS:
Bandido . . .
SEBASTIAN: (*Hands up.*)
You can have anything you want.

(*Kalibanos smiles broadly.*)

TRINC: (*Hands up.*)
We're from the boat. Yacht-o. Storm-o.
SEBASTIAN:
Wreck-o. Sink-o.
KALIBANOS:
Kalibanos.
SEBASTIAN:
You're Greek!
TRINC:
Acropolis.
SEBASTIAN:
Parthenon. Birth of Democracy.
TRINC:
Melina Mercouri . . . Telly Savalas . . . Kojak.
KALIBANOS:
Telly Savalas! Kojak. I like Kojak very much.
TRINC:
He speaks English!
SEBASTIAN:
He's kind of attractive in a third world kind of way.
KALIBANOS:
You want drink good stuff?

(*He goes to get the bottle of champagne, hands it to Sebastian, who takes a swig.*)

SEBASTIAN:
You have a good wine cellar.
TRINC:
The party is picking up.
SEBASTIAN:
Good wine—vintage Alonzo.
KALIBANOS:
You want to buy dirty statues?

(*Kalibanos leads them to a table covered with a heavy spread. He yanks a pulley to reveal the statues: A dozen figures with giant penises. Sebastian is overwhelmed.*)

KALIBANOS:
They are very old . . . antique . . .
TRINC:
You got something a little smaller?

EXT. PATH—WIDE SHOT—BEACH

(*A strange procession walking up the beach. Alonzo supported by the two sailors; Harry supporting Dolores still clutching her harp; Freddie, Aretha, Miranda and lastly Antonia. Phillip looks at her, then goes back to the front of the line and leads them to some rocks where they sit and rest.*)

DOLORES:
. . . Oh Harry. Wouldn't it be wonderful if we stayed here forever? We'd find ways to shelter ourselves from the elements. We could start an ideal society. No wars, no poverty. No traffic jams . . .
HARRY:
As a matter of fact, this spot might make a good Club Med.
DOLORES:
But that would ruin it.
HARRY:
Put in a decent harbor. Set up a marina. Half a dozen good, solid restaurants. An olympic size pool.
ALONZO:
Shut up, Harry.
PHILLIP: (*With authority.*)
Harry, you're free to say what you want. Alonzo is not the master of this island.
HARRY:
Who's the boss here?
PHILLIP:
Harry, can't you live without a boss?

HARRY:
Probably not. I like taking orders.
ARETHA:
Then you're in the right place.
HARRY:
Are you the big guy here, Phil?
PHILLIP:
Aretha, go up to the house and start a fire.
ARETHA:
Yes, Master.
FREDDIE:
Can I help?
ARETHA:
Ask the guy in the kimono . . . He's the one with the electricals . . .
PHILLIP:
Sure . . . go with her.
MIRANDA:
I'll go, too.
PHILLIP: (*Angry.*)
No. You stay with us.
MIRANDA:
I'm going.
ARETHA:
Let her come!

(*Aretha, Freddie and Miranda go up the hill. Antonia steps up to Phillip and looks after them.*)

ANTONIA:
There seems to be some question of authority on this island.
PHILLIP: (*Shouts.*)
Put some food on!
ARETHA: (*Shouts.*)
Okay!!
PHILLIP: (*To Antonia.*)
She's growing up. (*Referring to Miranda.*)
ANTONIA:
Did she . . . Did she talk about me?
PHILLIP:
Truthfully? . . . No.
ANTONIA:
Does she hate me?
PHILLIP:
Ask her yourself.

ALONZO:
Do you hate us, Phillip?
PHILLIP:
Yes, but I haven't really given it much thought.
ANTONIA:
I don't believe you.
PHILLIP:
Conscious thought.
ALONZO:
What the hell have you been doing then?
PHILLIP:
Waiting for you, sweetheart. (*Shouts.*) Kalibanos!!
ALONZO:
Who is Kalibanos?
PHILLIP:
Your long lost ancestor. (*Calls.*) Kalibanos.

EXT. PATIO—NIGHT

(*Miranda is hanging a kerosene lantern in a tree as Freddie steadies her. Aretha holds up another lantern for them to see better. Freddie helps Miranda down, and Aretha leads the way across the patio.*)

FREDDIE:
Best I ever surfed was the pipeline in Honolulu.
MIRANDA:
I've never been in Hawaii.
FREDDIE:
I went to school there for half a term. Didn't do much studying, so my old man shipped me to this military academy in Vermont.
ARETHA:
Oh, Vermont . . . Do they still have snow in Vermont?
FREDDIE:
Only in the winter, Ma'am. (*He sets a table upright for her.*)
ARETHA:
Thanks, Sonny. (*She goes into the kitchen.*)
FREDDIE:
I would've gone to public school but my old man wouldn't let me.
MIRANDA:
Why not?
FREDDIE:
I guess he doesn't really want me around full-time.

(*Freddie holds the lantern while Miranda picks up a flower pot.*)

MIRANDA:
Oh, thanks . . . What about my mother?
FREDDIE:
Antonia? . . . She's nice.
MIRANDA:
No. I mean, did she want you around full-time?
FREDDIE:
Well, she likes me. But my old man is the chief honcho.
MIRANDA:
Did she talk about me?
FREDDIE:
All the time.

(*Miranda turns and heads for the kitchen.*)

MIRANDA:
What did she say? . . . Watch your head.

(*Freddie follows her in.*)

FREDDIE:
A lot of love stuff . . . she didn't tell me you were beautiful.
MIRANDA:
Shut up please.
FREDDIE:
Did I say something wrong?

(*Aretha smiles, turns to Freddie.*)

ARETHA:
Do you think your people like Feta?
FREDDIE:
What's Feta? (*He tastes it.*) I hope so.
ARETHA:
Listen . . . why don't you go up and light some lights.

(*Miranda leads Freddie up into the room beyond.*)

MIRANDA:
. . . Sorry I said shut up.
FREDDIE:
Nice place you got here . . . All I said is you're beautiful.
MIRANDA:
I'm not exactly beautiful. Besides, I'm a virgin.

(*She shines a flashlight at the steep ladder, and Freddie climbs up ahead.*)

INT. BEDROOM—NIGHT

(*Freddie climbs up into the bedroom, turns to help Miranda. Miranda goes to the large lamp hanging in a corner of the room. Freddie holds up the chimney while she lights it. It takes all their concentration, and when it is lit, they both look at it in silence.*)

MIRANDA:
I've never been in love.
FREDDIE:
Neither have I . . .

(*Freddie kisses her, ever so gently. Miranda barely moves.*)

MIRANDA:
I'm not on the pill, so I guess that's all there is.

(*He kisses her again. He leans back. Then, she leans to Freddie and kisses him. Only the hissing of the lantern is heard.*)

EXT. PATHWAY

(*The group is closer to the house now. We see the lantern in Phillip's hand. He is leading Antonia down the path, at the head of the line.*)

ANGLE ON ANTONIA AND PHILLIP

PHILLIP:
Careful . . . watch your step.
ANTONIA:
I can't imagine you here for a whole year.
PHILLIP:
It's been very productive.
ANTONIA:
No pain?
PHILLIP:
Pure pleasure.
ANTONIA:
I don't believe you.
PHILLIP:
I don't care what you believe or don't believe.
ANTONIA:
Oh, really? What are you getting so angry about if you don't care what I believe?

(*They stop. The others walk past them.*)

PHILLIP:
Because I found paradise. Now you've turned it into a slum.
ANTONIA:
You've lost none of your pride I see.
PHILLIP:
I did the best I could.
ANTONIA:
Only for yourself.
PHILLIP:
The same as you then.
ANTONIA:
Always blame the other guy, as usual.
PHILLIP:
I was empty.
ANTONIA:
What the hell was I then?
PHILLIP:
I don't care what you were . . . what did you want from me?
ANTONIA:
I wanted us to share a life . . . I didn't want to just be part of yours, I didn't want to just stand there, you know . . . I wanted you to make some sacrifices, too!
PHILLIP: (*Quietly.*)
You want sacrifice? I'll give you sacrifice.

(*He goes toward the house. After a moment, Antonia picks up the lantern and follows him.*)

EXT./INT. COTTAGE

(*Phillip goes into the house, past Miranda and Freddie . . . and Aretha handing out blankets, helping Alonzo to a chair. Phillip goes to the patio in the back of the house . . . He leads the pet goat into the kitchen and closes the back door. He returns to the front of the house. All are assembled now, their faces lit by the light of the lanterns.*)

PHILLIP:
Your lives were spared. That's a miracle. On this island, we honor a miracle with a sacrifice.

(*Group stares in disbelief at Phillip. Phillip goes back in the kitchen. Aretha rushes in after him. Phillip takes a knife from the table, kneels and brings it down sharply to the throat of the goat.*)

GROUP

(*Miranda stares . . . Antonia . . . even Alonzo is stunned. The group reacts as we hear the sound of the goat bleating.*)

WIDE ANGLE

(*The group. . . . Not a move, not a sound . . . then Phillip picks up the dead goat and carries it away.*)

DISSOLVE TO:

EXT. HOUSE—NIGHT

(*CLOSE on Miranda's cassette player . . . Pull back as Aretha sets it down on the wall and pushes the button. The music is the tango Miranda danced to on the tower. Sexy, sad . . . Dolores and Harry, who are standing nearby, start to dance. Aretha smiles and heads for the outside stairs leading to the terrace. Dolores and Harry tango into the kitchen, and lead us to Miranda and Antonia.*)

ANTONIA:
Can I kiss you, Mush?

(*Miranda puts her arms around her mother.*)

MIRANDA:
I love you, Mommy.

(*CAMERA PANS up to the terrace, just as Aretha arrives from the stairs. Phillip is sitting at the fire he built, turning the goat on a spit. He is very sad.*)

ARETHA:
Hi, boss . . .
PHILLIP:
Hi, kid . . .

(*She comes up behind him and puts her arms around him.*)

ARETHA:
It's time to forgive.
PHILLIP:
Are you my teacher or my pupil?
ARETHA:
I'm just a nice Catholic girl from New Jersey, destined to roam the earth in search of Mister Nice . . . Meantime, you want to dance?

(They kiss and start to dance. They move to the edge of the terrace, and CAMERA once again pans along the outside of the house, down toward the kitchen window below.)

ANGLE ON ALONZO AND FREDDIE IN THE KITCHEN

ALONZO:
Freddie, could I ask you a question?
FREDDIE:
Sure, Pop.
ALONZO:
Would you be angry if I kissed you?
FREDDIE:
I don't think so.

(They embrace. Then Freddie looks through the open door to the patio.)

FREDDIE:
Excuse me, Dad . . .

(Freddie goes out to where Miranda is sitting on the wall overlooking the patio. CAMERA follows to the rhythm of the tango.)

FREDDIE:
You want to dance?

(Miranda smiles at him, and he leads her down to the patio. They dance. Alonzo comes down to watch them.)

ARETHA: *(To Alonzo.)*
Looks like Roseland on a slow night.
ALONZO:
Thank you for saving my life.
ARETHA:
Oh, it's nothing . . . Care to trip the light fantastic?
ALONZO:
I'd be delighted!

(He lifts her off the steps.)

ALONZO:
I like the way you sing.
ARETHA:
I like the way you lift.

(*They dance off together as Phillip comes down the steps and stops in front of Antonia.*)

PHILLIP:
So . . . how's baseball?
ANTONIA:
There was a baseball strike.
PHILLIP:
Oh yeah, I dreamt that . . . How's the cat?
ANTONIA:
Pregnant.
PHILLIP:
Forgive me.

(*Antonia looks at him for a moment. Then she jumps off the rock she's been standing on, and reaches for his arm.*)

ANTONIA:
Okay.

(*They start to tango.*)

PHILLIP:
Just like that?
ANTONIA:
I love you.

(*Suddenly the sound of drunken singing is heard. Kalibanos, Trinc and Sebastian stagger down the steps to the patio. Kalibanos is wearing Harry's western hat.*)

TRINC: (*Singing.*)
Should old acquaintance be forgot,
Be forgot, be forgot . . .
Fish and goats and goats and booze
Is what we got, is what we got.

(*Everybody cheers their arrival. There are greetings and hugs. Kalibanos suddenly seems transfixed. He reverently takes off the hat and walks off in the direction of Dolores. He taps Harry on the shoulder.*)

KALIBANOS:
May I cut in?
HARRY:
Hey, that's my hat, isn't it? My Stetson. Where did you find that?

(Kalibanos spirits Dolores away, leaving Harry still marveling at his reunion with his hat. Trinc comes over to Harry. They embrace and Trinc starts to dance.)

HARRY:
Hey, don't get any ideas, Arnie . . .

(Trinc looks up at him adoringly as they dance off.)

TRINC:
It's lonely in the cave.

(Sebastian has been eyeing Luigi [the sailor], sitting alone at a table.)

SEBASTIAN:
Would you care to dance?
LUIGI:
Grazie.

(Luigi rises and dances off with Sebastian, cheek to cheek.)

ANGLE ON DOLORES AND KALIBANOS

(Dancing close . . . you can feel the heat.)

KALIBANOS:
I am Kalibanos.
DOLORES:
I am Dolores.
KALIBANOS:
I like your melones.
DOLORES:
Thank you.
KALIBANOS: *(Husky-voiced with sexuality.)*
And your bumba.
DOLORES:
You're so strong, so beautifully primitive . . . What's a bumba?

(Kalibanos answers her question by squeezing the cheeks of her behind. She giggles.)

DOLORES:
You have charisma.
KALIBANOS:
My charisma is growing like a mountain flower in spring time.
DOLORES:
You're a poet?

KALIBANOS:
I am a singer.
PHILLIP: (*Dancing past Kalibanos.*)
Kalibanos.
KALIBANOS:
Yes, Phil?
PHILLIP:
Forgive me.
KALIBANOS:
For what, Phil?
PHILLIP:
Just forgive me.
KALIBANOS:
Okay, okay, okay . . .

(*Kalibanos dances off with Dolores, Phillip dances off with Antonia. As the tango continues, each couple in a special world of their own, the CAMERA slowly begins to rise, until it emcompasses the entire patio and the house. Everyone is dancing. Slowly, CAMERA moves through the branches of the olive trees, which begin to obscure the tango.*)

DISSOLVE TO:

EXT. ISLAND FROM SEA—FIRST LIGHT—DAWN

(*Mist slowly rising and revealing the island. We are MOVING AWAY FROM the land . . . on the same boat that brought them there.*)

BOAT—CLOSE ON FACE OF VASSILI

(*The same boatsman.*)

VASSILI:
We have a lot of islands here . . . Paros, Anafi. Santorini. Simos . . .

(*CAMERA PANS to others on the old fishing boat. Phillip . . . Miranda . . . Antonia.*)

VASSILI:
Milos, Serifos, Ikaria, Patmos, Rhodos, Gythio . . .

ANGLE ON BOAT

(*They are all looking at the island.*)

VASSILI:
Andros, Hios, Lesbos, Limnos . . .

ANTONIA:
I'm dreaming.
PHILLIP:
I know.

ANGLE ON MIRANDA

(*She sees something and is delighted.*)

HER POV

(*Freddie, in scuba gear, pops up from beneath sea and swims toward boat.*)

ANGLE ON FREDDIE

FREDDIE:
Hey . . . You never gave me your phone number.

ANGLE ON BOAT

MIRANDA:
Uh . . . Area code 212 . . . 555 . . . uh . . .
PHILLIP:
555-4499.
FREDDIE:
. . . 99. I'll call you.

(*Freddie disappears beneath the sea.*)

ANGLE ON BOAT

(*Miranda smiles.*)

ANGLE ON BOAT

(*They all stare at the island.*)

ISLAND—POV SHOT

(*Island disappearing from view, ever so slowly . . . almost fading away.*)

BOAT

(*As it disappears . . .*)

THE END

PHILLIP, MIRANDA, AND ANTONIA IN LIVINGROOM

MIRANDA AND PHILLIP ON ROOFTOP OF APARTMENT

KALIBANOS IN THE AMPHITHEATRE

ARETHA, OWNER, AND PHILLIP IN CAFE

PHILLIP AND DOG ON ISLAND

LAUNCH CAPSIZES AT SEA

KALIBANOS PLAYS TO THE GOATS

ALONZO AND ANTONIA ON LAUNCH